Amazing Trading Plans

Amazing Trading Plans

Don't Place Another Trade Without It!

Stephen Pierce

Impulsive Profits, Inc.
Ann Arbor, Michigan

ISBN 1-932448-05-5

Printed in the United States of America.

© Impulsive Profits, Inc. 2232 S. Main Street #421 Ann Arbor, Michigan 48103-6938
Phone 734-741-8392   Fax 734-741-8393

To my Lord Jesus Christ, without whom none of this would be possible. To Alicia, my lovely wife who has made my life complete.

Acknowledgements

I would like to thank the following people who were instrumental in either the creation of Amazing Trading Plans or in the support of the body of work at Impulsive Profits, Inc. My personal Lord and Savior Jesus Christ from which I draw my wisdom and direction; my dear wife Alicia, whose love frees me to create; all the wonderful family and staff at Impulsive Profits, Lorette Lyttle, Teddy Watts, Mom Lyttle, and Jennifer Podgorny; all of our clients around the world who motivate us to continue to strive to give our best.

For their unselfish contributions to this work; Rich Swannell, Michael Johnson, Jim Robinson, Bob DiMattia, Mark McRae, Mark Soberman, Earik Beann, Rich Creal, and Zoran.

Special thanks go to my brother Thomas "Pakii" Pierce, my best friends Richard Schefren and John Reese. Also to my mentor Mike Murdock whose friendship, mentorship and insights continue to inspire me to take action that makes a difference.

Table Of Contents

INTRODUCTION

By Stephen Pierce

The art of trading successfully comes from a combination of trying, failing, testing, trying again, failing again, evolving your mindset, repeating winning habits and patterns while persisting through the inevitable losses while keeping them as small as possible.

Losing trades are par for the course; however, most traders have not learned how to deal mentally, emotionally and financially with losing.

One of the best ways to deal with losing is to have solid trading plans that win more often than they loose. Or at the minimum, the winning trades bank more than the losing trades lose, thus giving you a net profit from your trading.

Okay, so that was not a revelation; however, having access to market tested trading plans that are solid in bull markets and bear markets that could make you consistently profitable if you follow them …well, they are hard to come by.

We have purchased every viable software program, trading course, advisory service and book that we felt had great potential as a solid trading plan, in order to find out what really works.

From this heap, finding solid trading plans was like looking for a needle in a hay stack. However, we did find some trading plans that are shockingly profitable, incredibly consistent and realistically tradable.

They are not without losses and they don't promise millions, but they are the simplest and easiest to follow amazing trading plans that you can use to start building your dream of trading at home for a living.

We have been fortunate enough to have some of the authors, advisors and traders we admire to contribute to this work we call **"Amazing Trading Plans"**.

In their own words, they will describe trading plans that they use for their trading services, sell in trading products and use personally to trade.

In addition, each month inside of the **Amazing Trading Plans VIP Access** area, we will introduce you to additional trading plans that fit under the umbrella of …*amazing!*

Each plan we detail for you each month will be done via multimedia streaming video so you can see the plan in full action. Many of the plans will be recorded during live intraday market action so you can see the trade unfold before your eyes to give you clarity on how to implement the strategy in your own trading.

With that said, let's begin your journey into what we feel you will agree with us to be…

…Amazing Trading Plans…

THE ULTIMATE TRADE SETUP

By Jim Robinson www.Profittrading.com

Markets move between low volatility trading range moves to high Volatility trend moves.

One of the best ways to see this taking place is with the Bollinger Bands. When a market makes a extremely narrow range move, the Bollinger Bands will noticeably narrow together.

When the bands narrow down it shows an extremely low volatility market. A low volatility market forecasts - a high volatility trend move is more than likely - just around the corner.

This is a big trading setup and a money making opportunity is at hand. The Bands narrowing together does not forecast the direction that the breakout will be but often times it is fairly clear from classic technical analysis which way the odds favor the breakout to be.

WHEAT - A NARROW RANGE BASE
At the beginning of the chart on the next page, from 3/20/03 to 5/06/03 Wheat made a narrow range base pattern.

The Bollinger Bands narrowed down and there was no doubt that a low volatility move was happening. This put us on alert that this was a Million Dollar trade setup. A possible trading opportunity was at hand and Wheat exploded to the upside from there.

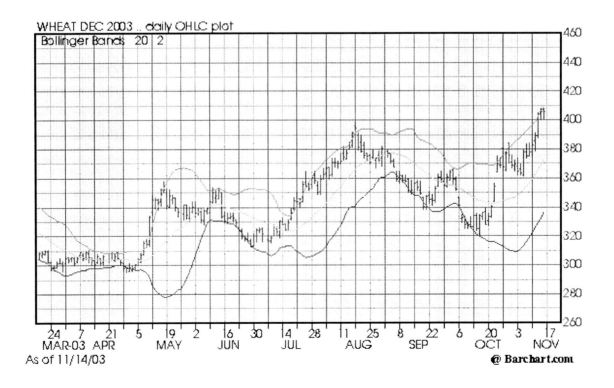

SOYBEANS - BLAST OFF!

On 8/08/03 The Bollinger Bands moved extremely close together and the trade setup stuck out like a sore thumb. There was no missing this one as Beans exploded above the bands and the rest is history.

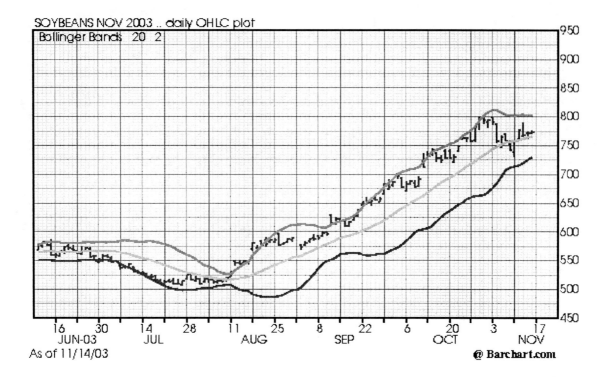

SOYBEANS NOV 2003 .. daily OHLC plot
Bollinger Bands 20 2
As of 11/14/03   @ Barchart.com

THE ENTRY SIGNAL

The parabolic stop indicator is a great way to make sure you are on board for the big move and a good indicator to use as a stop.

Sometimes it takes a couple of tries to get aboard the big move with the parabolic. The parabolic is a stop and reverse trading system.

The parabolic will work excellent as an entry signal then use the parabolic stop and reverse signal to change positions in the market if need be. So you use the parabolic to:

1. Enter the market.
2. As a stop if wrong on the entry signal.
3. As a new entry point to go with the market the other direction if need be.

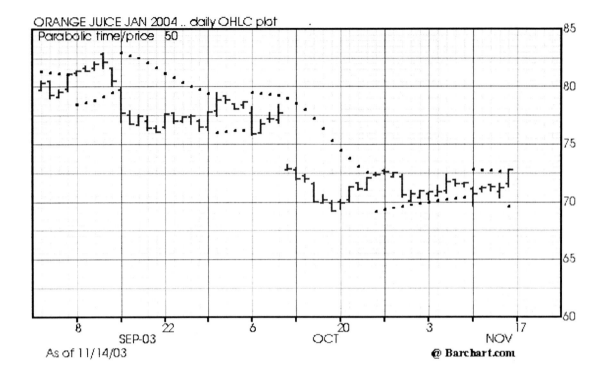

The reason it may take a couple tries to get in the market on the right side of the big trend move is because the market may make a false breakout.

For example the market may make a base and be ready to make a strong rally, but first the market may make a strong move below the base.

This is called a false breakout or head fake. Then the real move may begin and the market will rally from there. The false breakout can be in either direction and sometimes there may be a couple of false moves.

FROM JOHN BOLLINGER - ON BOLLINGER BANDS

Years ago the late Bruce Babcock of Commodity Traders Consumers Review interviewed me for that publication.

After the interview we chatted for a while--the interviewing gradually reversed--and it came out that his favorite commodity trading approach was the volatility breakout.

I could hardly believe my ears. Here is the fellow who had examined more trading systems--and done so rigorously--than anyone with the possible exception of John Hill of Futures Truth and he was saying that his approach of choice to trading was the volatility-breakout system, the very approach that I thought best for trading after a lot of investigation.

Perhaps the most elegant direct application of Bollinger Bands is a volatility breakout system. These systems have been around a long time and exist in many varieties and forms. The earliest breakout systems used simple averages of the highs and lows, often shifted up or down a bit. As time went on, average true range was frequently a factor.

There is no real way of knowing when volatility, as we use it now, was incorporated as a factor. One would surmise that one day someone noticed that breakout signals worked better when the averages, bands, envelopes, etc., were closer together and the volatility breakout system was born. (Certainly the risk-reward parameters are better aligned when the bands are narrow, a major factor in any system.)

Our version of the venerable volatility breakout system utilizes Bandwidth to set the precondition and then takes a position when a breakout occurs. There are two choices for a stop/exit for this approach.

First, Welles Wilder's Parabolic3 is a simple, but elegant concept. In the case of a stop for a buy signal, the initial stop is set just below the range of the breakout formation and then incremented upward each day the trade is open. Just the opposite is true for a sell. For those willing to pursue larger profits than those afforded by the relatively conservative Parabolic approach, a tag of the opposite band is an excellent exit signal. This allows for corrections along the way and results in longer trades. So, in a buy use a tag of the lower band as an exit and in a sell use a tag of the upper band as an exit.

The major problem with successfully implementing Method I is something called a head fake--discussed in the prior chapter. The term came from hockey, but it is familiar in many other arenas as well. The idea is a player with the puck skates up the ice toward an opponent.

As he skates he turns his head in preparation to pass the defender; as soon as the defenseman commits, he turns his body the other way and safely snaps his shot. Coming out of a Squeeze, stocks often do the same; they'll first feint in the wrong direction and then make the real move.

Typically what you'll see is a Squeeze, followed by a band tag, followed in turn by the real move. Most often this will occur within the bands and you won't get a breakout signal until after the real move is under way. However, if the parameters for the bands have been tightened, as so many who use this approach do, you may find yourself with the occasional small whipsaw before the real trade appears.

Some stocks, indices, etc are more prone to head fakes than others. Take a look at past Squeezes for the item you are considering and see if they involved head fakes. Once a faker…

For those who are willing to take a non-mechanical approach trading head fakes, the easiest strategy is to wait until a Squeeze occurs--the precondition is set--then look for the first move away from the trading range. Trade half a position the first strong day in the opposite direction of the head fake, adding to the position when the breakout occurs and using a parabolic or opposite band tag stop to keep from being hurt.

Where head fakes aren't a problem, or the band parameters aren't set tight enough for those that do occur to be a problem, you can trade Method I straight up. Just wait for a Squeeze and go with the first breakout.

Volume indicators can really add value. In the phase before the head fake look for a volume indicator such as Intraday Intensity or Accumulation Distribution to give a hint regarding the ultimate resolution. MFI is another indicator that can be useful to improve success and confidence. These are all volume indicators and are taken up in Part IV.

The parameters for a volatility breakout system based on The Squeeze can be the standard parameters: 20-day average and +/- two standard deviation bands. This is true because in this phase of activity the bands are quite close together and thus the triggers are very close by. However, some short-term traders may want to shorten the average a bit, say to 15 periods and tighten the bands a bit, say to 1.5 standard deviations.

There is one other parameter that can be set, it is the look-back period for the Squeeze. The longer you set the look-back period--recall that the default is six months--the greater the compression you'll achieve and the more explosive the set ups will be. However, there will be fewer of them. There is always a price to pay it seems.

Method 1 first detects compression through The Squeeze and then looks for range expansion to occur and goes with it. An awareness of head fakes and volume indicator confirmation can add significantly to the record of this approach. Screening a reasonable size universe of stocks--at least several hundred--ought to find at least several candidates to evaluate on any given day.

Look for your Method I setups carefully and then follow them as they evolve. There is something about looking at a large number of these setups, especially with volume indicators, that instructs the eye and thus informs the future selection process as no hard and fast rules ever can.

100% AUTOMATIC BOLLINGER BAND SYSTEM
All of this information works for Stocks and (or) Commodities.

THE BUY SIGNAL
1. Wait for the Bollinger Bands to make narrow range.
2. Wait for a close above the Bollinger Bands.
3. Buy when the high of the day that closed above the bands is taken out (Traded above).
4. Put a stop if wrong at the low of the day that closed above the bands.
5. So we're risking one bar of trading action.

THE SELL SIGNAL

1. Wait for the Bollinger Bands to make a narrow range.
2. Wait for a close below the Bollinger Bands.
3. Sell when the 1 day low is taken out - (traded below).
4. Put a stop if wrong at the high of the day that closed below the bands.
5. So we're risking one bar of trading action.

Take the general idea behind this system and change it anyway that works best for you. This is just an idea for you to build on.

STOCKS

Here are some examples of stocks making a narrow range and then a strong move.

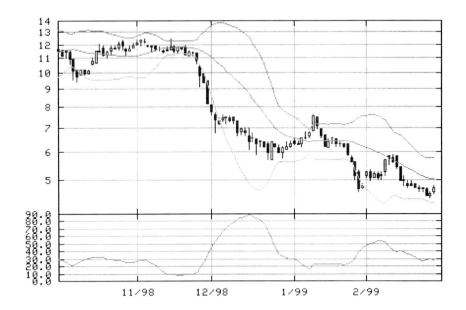

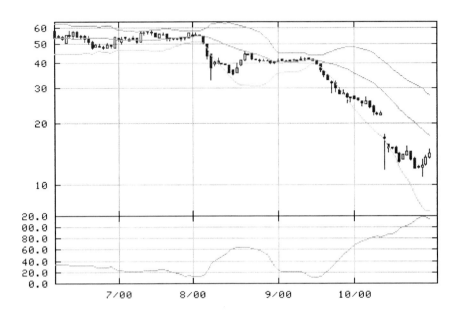

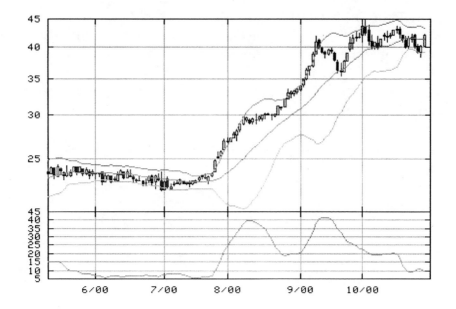

A COUPLE MORE COMMODITY CHART EXAMPLES

I did the following write up before Natural Gas broke-out to the upside. This chart of Natural Gas (next page) is making a narrow range.

We could start taking parabolic buy and sell signals until we caught the trend or we could wait for a breakout and look for the bands to expand.

That would show us the direction of the breakout. Then we could hop aboard in the direction of the trend.

Since Natural Gas has been in a downtrend and is making a base and has an Elliott Wave 3-4-5 wave bottom look to it, odds favor that this market will explode to the upside.

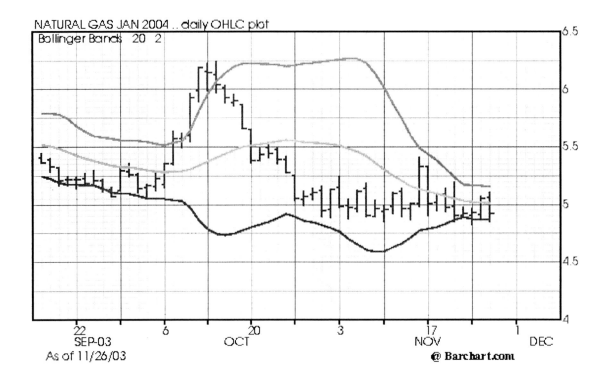

Here's what has happened since the above was written. Natural Gas has exploded to the upside.

Notice how The Bollinger Bands went from narrow range (Low Volatility) and are expanding with the rally (High Volatility). This gives us a lot of trading information.

1. A Major Low is most likely in - this market should continue to rally.
2. Since the bands expanded as the market rallied the trend should continue much higher from here.
3. We can buy corrections in this market from here.

Of course we have to monitor the market on a daily basis as any of this can change at any time. But as today the above market analysis is good. A low is in - we're long - stay bullish. If you're not in yet - look for places to buy and as always use a stop if wrong on all trades.

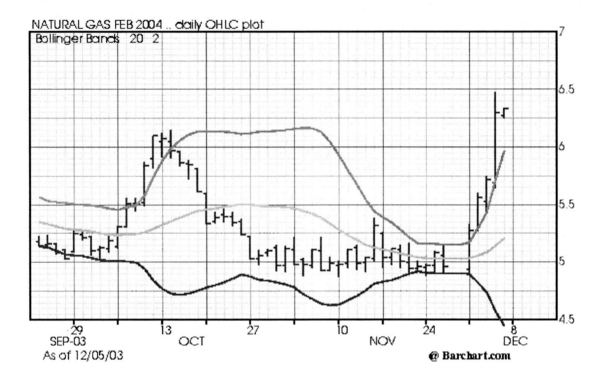

So this is not something that works just in hind site, this works in real time.

On the first chart of Natural Gas we were looking to buy a breakout when Natural Gas closed above the Bollinger Bands.

In my daily commodity newsletter I recommended to buy just above the breakaway day's high with a stop if wrong just below the breakaway day's low
and this trade setup worked like a charm.

TRADING TRICK
O.K. Natural Gas is in a new bull market or at least probably going to rally for awhile. (It could be any Stock or Commodity - Natural Gas is just an example).

Let's say you didn't buy at the lows but with the big rally you have turned extremely bullish.

Here's a good way to find entry levels from here.

> Look for the 14 day stochastic to move to oversold - a reading below 30.
> An oversold 14 day stochastic reading is often where corrections will end.
> This will be where the market will normally rally from (if the rally continues).

> ➢ Take buy signals - with a close stop if wrong.

Here is a Lean Hog Example

This chart of Lean Hogs made a narrow range move right at 50 before the sharp bull swing to 60.

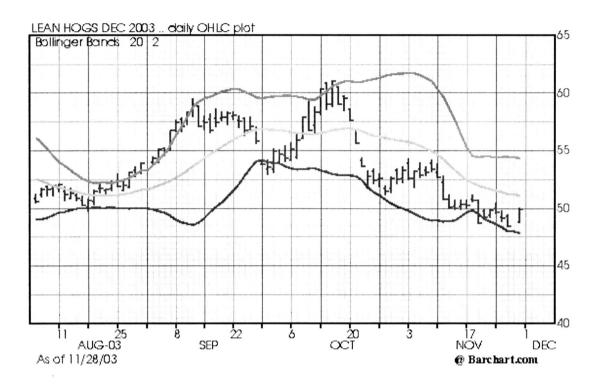

The breakout above the Bollinger Bands was an excellent place to get long for the rally.

I wrote up the first part of plan around the end of November 2003. Here is a current trade we took this week in Sugar.

> ➢ Sugar closed below the 10-8 trading bands on Wednesday 2/04/04.
> ➢ A move below Wednesday's low was a good try to get short.
> ➢ The low Wednesday was 5.77, so we were selling at 5.76.
> ➢ Thursday Sugar gapped down and opened at 5.65.
> ➢ So we were short from 5.65, with a stop if wrong, just above Tuesday's high of 5.85. So the stop if wrong was 5.86.
> ➢ Friday Sugar gapped down and closed at 5.45.
> ➢ So as of today Saturday 2/07/04, we are short from 5.65 and have moved our stop if wrong to breakeven 5.65.

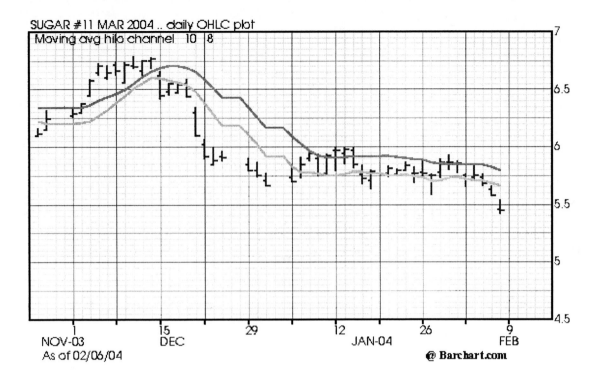

Whenever a market is in a narrow trading range it presents a good trading opportunity because the breakaway normally turns into a strong trend move.

The Bollinger Bands showed the narrow range. The upper and lower bands moved together as market volatility contracted. Sugar has broke lower and is trading below the Bollinger Bands and that says loud and clear the breakaway was to the downside.

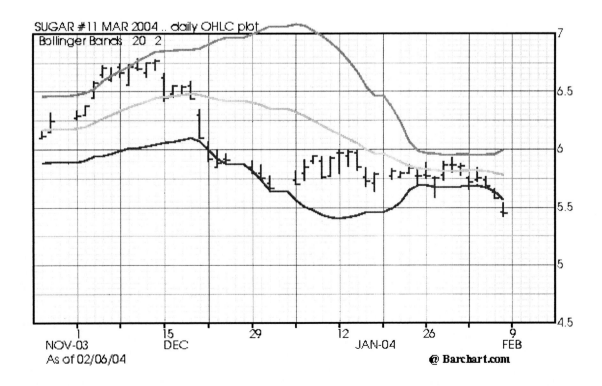

The Volatility indicator made a straight line as Sugar traded sideways.

The Volatility indicator was on a sell signal during the trading range so the Volatility indicator put the odds with the downside.

If Sugar traded higher and triggered a Volatility buy signal then the breakaway would have been to the upside.

Notice how when Sugar broke lower the Volatility indicator moved lower. You could use the down move in The Volatility indicator as a sell signal whenever a market goes into a sideways range - even a short term range.

The Volatility indicator is a good indicator to keep an eye on.

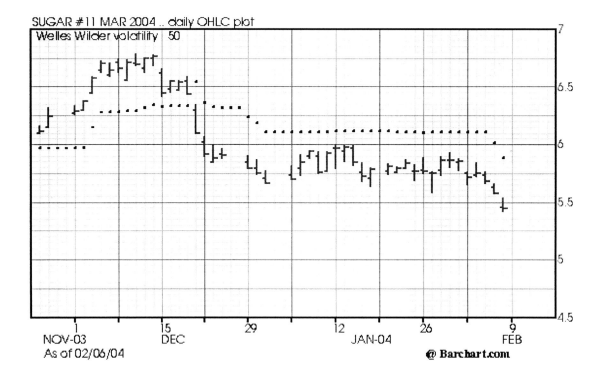

The parabolic indicator was already on a sell signal. As Sugar narrowed down
that signaled the breakaway would be to the downside.

If the parabolic would have put in a buy signal then the breakaway might have been to
the upside

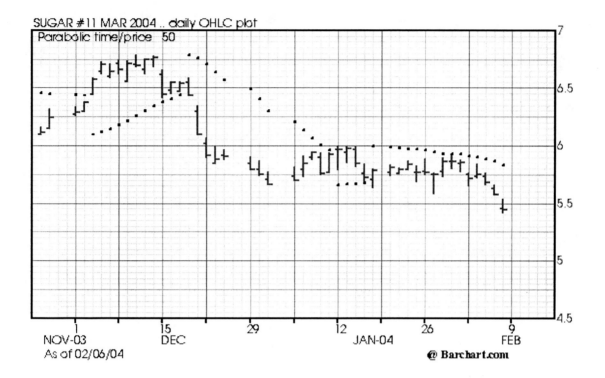

Here's a few more charts we were looking at to make our decision to go short Sugar.

The Keltner Channels showed the downtrend. A move below the Keltner Channels is bearish and says lower prices ahead.

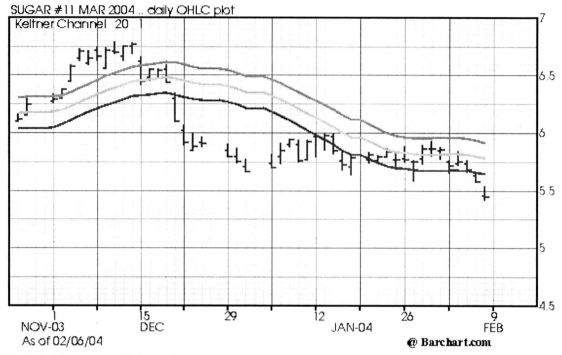

The 4-9-18 exponential moving averages showed a downtrend and told us odds favor a breakaway to the downside.

The Simple Profitable Trading Method
By Mark McRae www.tradingforbeginners.com

The method of trading I am going to cover in the pages to come are designed for the forex market. I have used it in other markets but it is designed primarily for the forex market.

One of the problems with designing a trading method, which is formed into a trading plan, is that one size does not fit all. I learned many years ago that I felt much more comfortable in slightly longer time frames than I did on very short time frames. With the method time frames can be adjusted for the individual so that it could be used as an intraday method or for much larger time frames.

Components of the Method

I am going to refrain from going too in-depth about each component of the method as there are plenty of good books and web sites on the individual subjects and most traders will be familiar with most of indictors used. The method consists of:

- Determining Trend
- Trend Indictor
- Fibonacci Ratios
- Multiple Time Frames

Determining Trend

I use good old exponential moving averages (EMA) for my primary trend identification in combination with at least one other time frame.

I also like big long moving averages as opposed to shorter time periods such as 5, 10 or 20 period moving averages. The reason I like the longer moving averages is that they are less inclined to whipsaw. Often with any combination of smaller moving averages you will find a lot of whipsaw.

For all time frames we will use an 89 period EMA of the highs and an 89 period EMA of the lows (89's). This is our short-term trend. Our long-term trend will be 144 period EMA of the highs and a 144 period's EMA of the lows (144's).

If the red 89's BOTH cross the black 144's then the trend is up and remains up unless both the red 89's cross below the black 144's. If the red 89's enter the price range of the black 144's the trend still remains up unless both red lines cross below the black lines.

The opposite is true for the trend to change from up to down. Have a look at the charts below.

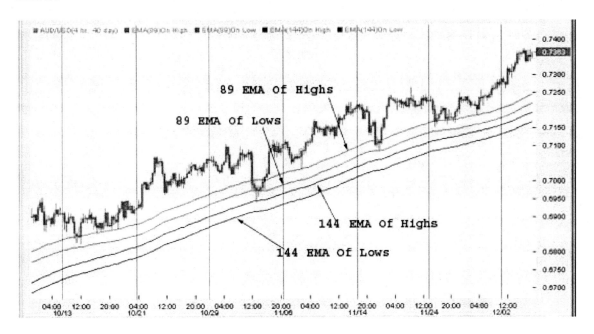

Trend Indictor

Although I use the EMA as to find my main trend direction there will be many rises and falls in price. To help determine when to enter and exit a trade I have a different indictor, which I call the trend indictor (TI). If the trend as determined by the EMA is up I will only take long trades and vice versa for short trades. The basis of the trend indictor is swing points.

Swing Point Up

A swing point "up" is when we have two higher highs than the "S" bar.

Swing Up

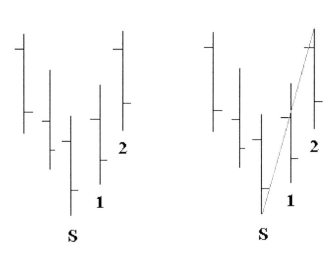

For the purpose of our swing points, we are not interested in the open or close of the bar. We are only interested in the high and low.

Take any bar on a chart and think of that as your starting point (S Bar). If you have two consecutive higher highs than the S bar then you have a swing up. If you don't have two higher highs then it is not a swing up and you do not mark it as an S bar.

Look at the diagram below. There are 13 bars but it was not until bar M that we actually had two consecutive higher highs than an S bar.

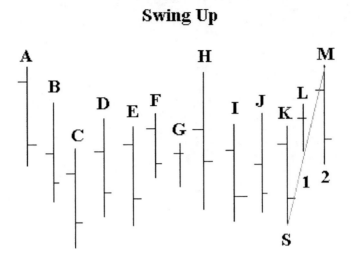

Swing Down

The reverse applies to the swing down. Use any starting point and name it the "S" bar. If you get two consecutive lower lows than the S bar then you have a swing down. If you do not get two consecutive lower lows after the S bar then it is not a valid S bar.

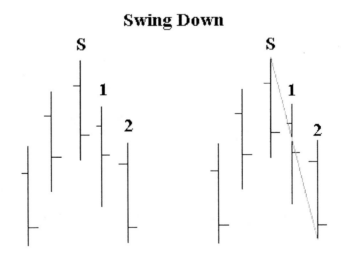

You can see from the diagram below that although there are 13 bars but we did not get a confirmed swing down until bar M.

Swing Down

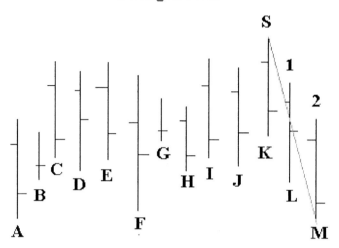

In an uptrend, the trend indictor can only change to down when the most recent valley (SU) has been breached.

In a downtrend, the trend indicator can only change to up when the most recent peak (SD) has been breached.

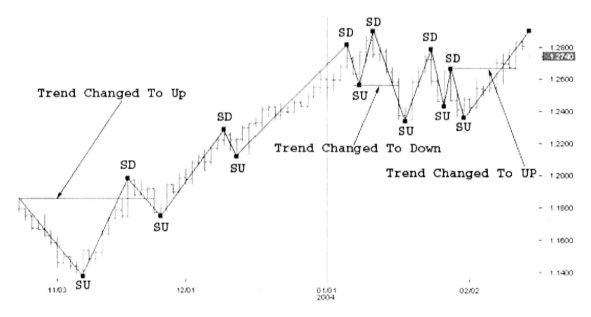

Fibonacci Ratios

Leonardo Fibonacci da Pisa was a mathematician born around 1170. He published his now famous Liber Abacci (Book of Calculation) in which amongst other things he comes up with the sequence of numbers.
1,1,2,3,5,8,13,34,55,89,144>>On to infinity

If you add one of the numbers in the sequence to the number before it, you get the next number in the sequence e.g. 3+5=8 and so on.

After the first few numbers in the sequence, if you measure the ratio of any number to that of the next higher number you get .618 e.g. 34 divided by 55 equals 0.618. The further along the sequence you go the closer to phi you will get.

If you measure the ratio between alternative numbers you get .382 e.g. 34 divided by 89 = 0.382 and that's about as far into the explanation as I care to go.

Now, although the three most popular Fibonacci ratios for trading are .382, .500 and .618, we will only be using .382 (38.2%) and .618 (61.8%) for our retracement calculations.

In an uptrend, measure the distance between point A and point B and in a downtrend measure the distance between point A and point B where point A is always the most recent swing up in an uptrend and the most recent swing down in a downtrend.

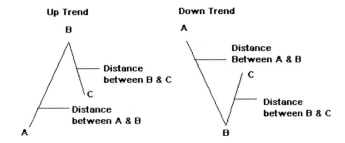

The next use of Fibonacci you will be applying is that of targets. You will always have three potential targets. Which target you select will depend on market condition and certain criteria.

Targets are calculated by measuring the distance between points A, B and C. Point C is the most recent low point of the retracement before the market moves up in an uptrend. In a downtrend it is the most recent high before the market continued down.

The calculations for targets are as follows.

Target 1
0.618*(Point B - Point A)+ Point C

Target 2
Point B – Point A + Point C

Target 3
1.618*(Point B – Point A)+ Point C

Multiple Time Frames

The idea behind this method of trading is to identify an opportunity on a higher time frame and then actually trade it on a smaller time frame. The time frames I use are a 4-hour for the main trend and a 30-minute chart for entry and exit. You could also use a 5-minute chart for entry and exit.

Putting It All Together

Long Trades

Rule #1
The 89's and the 144's on the 4–hour chart and on the 30–minute chart must both be in buy mode. By buy mode I mean that at some point the 89's have crossed over the 144's.

Rule #2
The TI (trend indicator) must be in buy mode on the 4-hour chart. The TI must just be changing from down to up or already be in buy mode.

Rule #3
Once these conditions have been met then we use the 30–minute chart for our entry, exit and target.

Rule #4
We only enter on a 38.2% retracement. You only place your stop loss under the 61.8% retracement and you only use the targets as calculated by the target formula.

Rule #5
You only select trades where the potential reward is at least twice the potential loss.

Short Trades

Rule #1
The 89's and the 144's on the 4–hour chart and on the 30–minute chart must both be in sell mode. By sell mode I mean that at some point the 89's have crossed below the 144's.

Rule #2
The TI (trend indicator) must be in sell mode. The TI must just be changing from up to down or already be in sell mode.

Rule #3
Once these conditions have been met then we use the 30–minute chart for our entry, exit and target.

Rule #4

We only enter on a 38.2% retracement. You only place your stop loss under the 61.8% retracement and you only use the targets as calculated by the targets formula.

Rule #5

You only select trades where the potential reward is at least twice the potential loss.

This is an example of the method at work. The first chart is of a 4 -hour EUR/USD.

The main trend as determined by the 89's and 144's on the 4-hour chart has been in buy mode for some time.

The TI was previously in a downtrend and on the 26th November 03 it changed back to an uptrend. The TI does not need to move from down to up or vice versa before you can trade. It does however need to be in the same direction at the time you enter the trade.

As it happened the TI turned up, so you would then go to your 30-minute chart to look for an entry.

If you look at the next chart, which is the 30-minute chart, the 89's and 144's were initially in sell mode.

Remember before you can trade both the 4-hour and 30-minutes charts, 89's and 144's must be in the same direction.

Once the 30–minute 89's and 144's moved into buy, you were then looking for a low point (support) to use as Point A. This is where you start your Fibonacci measurements.

I use low and high points, which are little areas of support and resistance. I don't use the swing points from the TI on the 30–minute chart. It can happen that they are the same points, but it is not a prerequisite. For smaller time frames I prefer just to use support and resistance areas.

When choosing point A to B, the more thrust (succession of higher highs and higher lows) there is the better.

You will always know where Point A is because you choose that point. Point B you will find quickly because it is fairly easy to see when the market has made a high (resistance) and is pulling back.

So you have Point A marked, which will often be the low point just before the TI changed and you mark Point B, which is the most recent high before the market pulled back. With these two points you then need to make some decisions.

You need to decide:
a)   Am I going to take this trade?
b)   Where am I going to enter, exit and target?

We have two points to work with – Point A and Point B. Point C hasn't been formed yet so you need to make an estimate of what your risk reward will be on the trade in order to make a decision.

What I do is to calculate the 38.2% retracement level as an estimate of what Point C might be. Let's work through this.

To start with Point A was 1.1794. This was the most recent low before the TI changed. The market formed minor resistance at 1.2040 and started pulling back to the EMA. From these two numbers I know that the 38.2% retracement level is 1.1946, which is our entry level.

We now have Point A and B and we are using the 38.2% Fibonacci retracement as our point C.

We can now calculate our targets using the formula mentioned previously:

Target 1
0.618*(Point B - Point A)+ Point C
0.618*(1.2040 – 1.1794) +1.1946 = 1.2098

Target 2
Point B – Point A + Point C
1.2040 – 1.1794 + 1.1946 = 1.2192

Target 3
1.618*(Point B – Point A)+ Point C
1.618*(1.2040 – 1.1794) + 1.1946 = 1.2344

With all this information you can now make a decision to trade or not. You know that the entry point will be 1.1946 with a stop loss just below 1.1888 and three possible targets from the calculation above. All the targets looked good with all of them offering a better than 2-1 return, so you can take the trade.

The market eventually pulled back to 1.1935. When marking Point C all you need to do is look for the lowest point (support) before the market starts back up again in an uptrend or starts back down again in a downtrend.

With Point C in place on 1st December 03, you can now go back and recalculate a new Point C. We originally used the 38.2% retracement level as Point C but with a new point C in place we have to recalculate the targets. The new calculation gave us a 1st target of 1.2087, a 2nd target of 1.2181 and a 3rd target of 1.2333.

You now have to choose which one of these targets you think the market will reach. Because the market had pulled back to the 89's on the 4–hour chart you can expect support in that area. As support had already formed you could assume that the market was ready for a move back up.

This would lead me to think that a larger target was in order - either a T2 or a T3. As T2 was going to be over 200 pips away and the T3 with the information we have was going to be close to 400 pips, the logical choice would be T2. The reason T2 seems logical is that 200 pips is achievable in a day or two but it is unlikely to move 400 pips in such a short time.

You now have this situation:

In the market at 1.1946
Stop Loss Order at 1.1888
Limit Order at 1.2181

With all the orders in place you just need to wait and see how the trade develops.
The T2 was hit on the 8th December 03 for a profit of 235 pips.
Mark McRae is the author of two ebooks Trading For Beginners
(www.tradingforbeginners.com) and Sure-Fire Forex Trading
(www.surefire-forex-trading.com). He can be reached at
info@surefire-forex-trading.com

Mark McRae
Suite 10
X0001
Balitto
4420
South Africa
0835444475

How To Trade The Markets Successfully
By Rich Creal, CTA   www.tradewithsuccess.com

In the many years I've been in the trading field, I've had the pleasure and privilege to meet a lot of nice people who trade. People from all walks of life: doctors, lawyers, sales people, police offers, stay-at-home mom and dads.

I've also been exposed to thousands of different trading methodologies, techniques and strategies: astrology, technical indicators, fundamental analysis, neuronet software, fuzzy logic programs, numerology, proprietary indicators.

My revolutionary conclusion:

99.9% of people trading are clueless about successful trading!

99.9% of the trading methodologies don't work!

After wasting way too much money on the next "secret" trading method and spending thousands of hours reading material on trading (which is 99.9% garbage), I finally realized I need to seek out true professional, successful traders whom are actually CONSISTENTLY MAKING MONEY.

So I knocked on numerous doors, sent countless emails, bugged people on the phone until I tracked down a pro trader who would actually show me what worked.

It took him less than 5 minutes!

You see, virtually all traders already have the knowledge to trade successfully. Buy low, sell high. Trading isn't complicated, you can only buy or sell. That's it!

Where losing traders screw up is they make things complicated!

Trading is simple! Tattoo that on your forehead.

I've had the privilege of watching and learning from true professionals, traders whom trade their own account and literally suck money from the market like a vacuum cleaner.

Each trader had his own methodology and twist on trading to suit his own personality, however there were FIVE DISTINCT TRAITS each trader shared.

So what are these five characteristics?

1. Keep things simple
2. Proper capitalization
3. Support and resistance
4. Multiple Time Frames
5. Prepare everyday

Let's talk about each one of these a bit further:

1 – Keep things simple

Trading can get complicated quickly. With all the different software packages, charting indicators, trade signal services and myths about the market, a trader can easily get stuck in analysis paralysis.

Have you ever seen a trader who had so many charting indicators on a chart you couldn't even see what was being traded? It's crazy.

The first rule is to keep things simple. Simply have enough rules for your trading to give you confidence to trade.

The key here is to trust your trading decisions. If you need 17 different things on your chart to confirm a trade, you are in serious trouble.

A moving average, a simple chart pattern, a new high, whatever. Keep it simple. Trust your ability and have confidence in your trading decisions.

2 – Proper capitalization

This is an area where most people blow it. You need money to trade. Trading money you are fearful of losing is called trading with "scared money" … a plan virtually guaranteed to cause failure.

You need enough money in your account to trade. If the minimum amount to trade is $5K, put $15K or $20K in the account. That doesn't mean you have to use it all. Trading already is stressful enough … you don't need the added worry of losing what little money you have in your account.

Proper capitalization also involves proper money management. There are several good works on money management. The key point here is a trader MUST balance risk-to-reward in order to succeed long term.

3 – Support and resistance

Each pro trader I met had a different methodology of trading, but each methodology used a form of support and resistance. The pro trader would determine support and resistance areas or levels and would use these for trade entries and exits.

After all, support and resistance (and all analysis techniques) simply validate an emotionally based decision to trade.

4 – Multiple Time Frames

No matter what time frame you trade, you need to be aware of what's going on larger time frames.

For example, if you trade 1 minute bar charts, be aware of what's happening on the 5 minute bar chart and 30 minute bar chart.

If you trade daily bar charts, be aware of what's happening on the weekly and monthly bar charts.

Charles Drummond, a famous trader, created the rule of 5s. This simply stated time-frames should be in multiples of 5. So if you trade the 1 minute chart, your other time frames would be 5 minutes and 25 minutes. I recommend this as a general rule, however you can round off the timeframes to suit your needs.

5 – Prepare everyday

Many traders fail to prepare themselves for trading on a daily basis. Each day is a new event, a separate and different time from previous trading days.

Focus on the day ahead of you. Remember what happened yesterday but don't dwell on it.

Clear your mind and keep focused on trading. If you aren't feeling well, have a life issue (sickness in the family, marital issues, etc.), you probably aren't in the right frame of mind. Do not trade.

A Simple Method I Use For Determining
Support and Resistance for Day Trading

While many methods of support and resistance exist, any method I use must meet four criteria:

1. It must be based upon mathematically based principles.
2. It must be duplicable.
3. It must be simple.
4. It must incorporate multiple time frames.

To determine support and resistance, I use volume at price. This simply means I determine support and resistance areas by the volume of trades at a particular price point.

The CBOT™ developed a highly effective tool for representing the volume at price called the Market Profile™.

The Market Profile™ displays a traded vehicle's volume for the previous day. (See CQG example below.)

```
                                                           O=   10903
11108 ·                                                    H=   10911
11107 ·                                                    L=   10822
11106 ·                                                    L=   10827ᵛ
11105 ·                                                    Δ=      +4
11104 ·
11103 ·
11102 · y
11101 ·→ y                               K
11100 · y                               DJK
11031 · y                               DEJKL
11030 · y                               DEFJKL
11029 · y                               DEFJKL◄
11028 · y                               DEFJKL
11027 · y                               CDEFGHJL
11026 · y                               CDEFGHIJ
11025 · y                               CDFGHIJ
11024 · y                               CDFGHI
11023 · y                               CDFGHI
11022 · y                               CFGHI
11021 · y                               CI
11020 · y                               C
11019 · y                               BC
11018 · yA                              BC            y
11017 · yzA                             BC            y
11016 · yzA                             BC            yz
11015 · zA                     F        BC            yz
11014 · zAB          z         F       ►B          →  yz
11013 · zAB          yz        FG       yB            yz
11012 · zABG         yz        FG       yzB           yz
11011 ·►zABCG        yz        FG       yzB           yz
11010 · zABCG        yzA       FG       yzB           yz
11009 · zABCFG       yzA       FG       yzB           yz
11008 · zACFG        yzA       FGH      yzAB          zA
11007 · zACEFGK      yzAB      FGH      yAB           zA
11006 · ACEFGK       yAB       ABFGH    yAB           zAB
11005 · ACDEFGKL     yAB       ABFH     yB            zAB
11004 · ACDEFGJKL◄   yAB       ABDFHIK  yB            zAB
11003 · ACDEFGJKL    yABD      ABDFHIK  yB            zB
11002 · CDEFGHJKL   ►yABDFI    ABDEFIK  B             B
11001 · DEFGHJKL     yABDFIJ  ►ABCDEFIJK  y           B
11000 · DEFGHJKL     yABDFGIJ  ABCDEFIJK→ y           B
10931 · DEFHJKL    → yBDEFGIJ  ABCDEFIJKL y           B
10930 · DFHIJK       BCDEFGHIJK zACDEJKL  y           B
10929 · DFHIJ        BCDEFGHIKL zACDEJKL  y           B
10928 · DFHIJ        BCDEFGHKL◄ zACDEJKL  y           B
10927 · DFHI         BCDEHKL    zAJL◄     y           B
10926 · FI           BCDEHK     zJL                   B
10925 · FI           BCDK       yz                    B
10924 · FI           C          yz                    B
10923 · FI           C          yz                    B
10922 · F                       yz                    B
10921 ·►F                       y                     B
10920 ·                        →y                    ►B
10919 ·                         y                     B
10918 ·                                               B
10917 ·                                               BC
10916 ·                                               BC
10915 ·                                               BC
10914                                                 BC
       11/21    11/22     11/25    11/26     11/27   11/29
```

Many different methods exist for using the Market Profile™, I use three items:

The Value Area (Upper Value Area and Lower Value Area) and the Point of Control.

The Value Area is the area which encloses 70% of the previous day's volume. The Point of Control it the price point which had the highest volume.

I also use the 10 day simple moving average of the close. This provides me a higher level view of what the market is doing. If the 10 day DMA is significantly away from the current price, I want to be aware of that. The 10 day DMA is the means, and price tends to gravitate towards the means.

(Example)

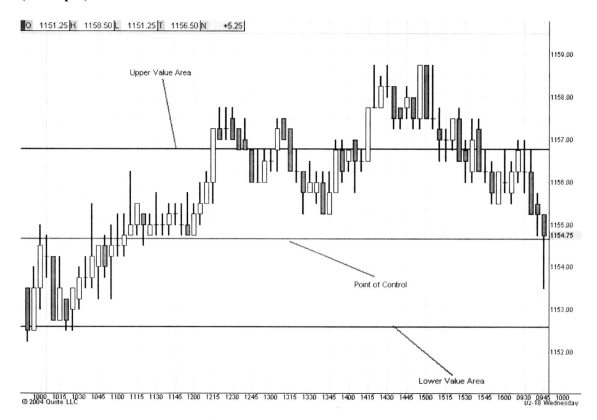

On this chart, we have the S&P 500 futures index e-mini (ES) charted on a 5 min. bar chart. The Upper Value Area, Lower Value Area, and Point Of Control are drawn:

UVA = 1156.72
LVA = 1152.60
POC = 1154.68

10 Day DMA = 1142.42.

Rules-of-thumb for using the Value Area

If price is above the Value Area, you want to be long. If price is below the Value Area, you want to be short. If the price is inside the Value Area, use the Point of Control for a pivot point. Above the POC, you want to be long. Below the POC, you want to be short.

Trading inside the Value Area is very short term (i.e. scalping) and you should not look for large moves, as you would on a breaking or rallying marketing outside the Value Area boundaries.

All of these points, Upper/Lower Value Area, POC and 10 DMA act as support and resistance areas. If the price is above one of these points, then the point acts as support. If the price is below one of these points, then the point acts as resistance. My (simple) analysis is this chart:

The close 1157.50 is significantly above the 10 DMA, so the market is slightly overbought. I want to favor short trades. The Value Area is small, so I'll look for a break outside of the Lower Value Area.

(Example)

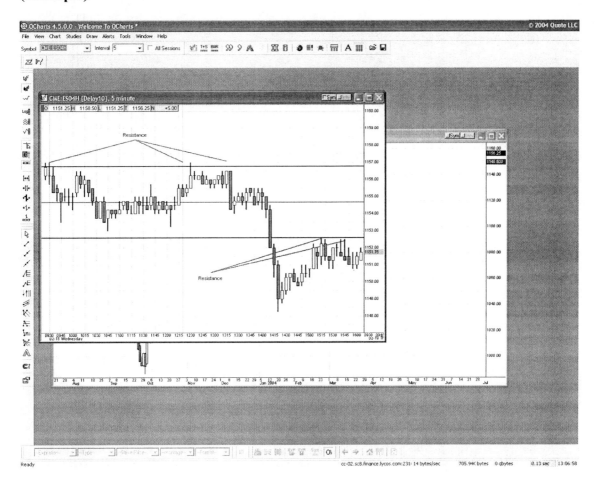

As you can see on this chart, the Upper Value Area acted as resistance several times throughout the session.

At 1400 hrs., the market broke and moved towards the Lower Value Area. The bar at 1410 hrs. closed at 1152.00, this would be my entry for a short trade.

This particular trade would probably be worth 1.5 – 3 points. This was a range bound day, so one cannot expect too much movement. There were several opportunities for trades earlier in the day (playing resistance off the Upper Value Area), however that's not my style of trading.

I look for larger moves, but take what the market will provide.

The Zoran Plan

By Zoran   www.truetrend.com

Two completely opposite "schools of thought" dominate today's public opinion when it comes to financial markets. One school of thought is advocated by academic types: mostly economics, finance and mathematics professors.

They will tell you that "markets are efficient" and that there is a zero chance for an individual to outperform any liquid financial market in the long run. Well, of course the guys with cushy university jobs, without any real world or business experience, will tell you that you don't stand a chance to succeed.

You should continue to work your little day job so that they have someone to make their sandwich or to change oil in their cars. People who subscribe to this theory usually chose to stay out of financial markets and keep their cash stashed in their mattresses.

Another school of thought is advocated by financial TV and radio stations, investment firms, brokerages etc… "Surprisingly" they are all trying to portray financial markets as an idyllic place where happy Moms, Dads and Grandpas use sophisticated software to place winning trades from their laptops while vacationing on sandy Caribbean beaches…

Countless "talking heads" are enjoying their daily parade on TV channels such as CNBC or CNN supplying mostly worthless advice to general public. Their "analysts" change their opinion every day in a fashion that even George Orwell would find hard to comprehend. And everything they say always seems to "make sense" at the moment when they are saying it.

Next day, when it turns out that they were totally wrong, they are telling you entirely different story as if yesterday never happened. And if you noticed, the hosts never, ever bring that up. Why? Well, "the show must go on". They have to show you that every day you are missing on countless trading opportunities; you just need to watch their shows, subscribe to fancy software that they sell you and you are on your way to early retirement.

I do agree with the statement that financial markets are efficient. They are very efficient in one thing - transferring money from bad and naive traders/investors to the pockets of those that know what are they doing.

A question that I hear the most from aspiring traders is "Which market should I trade? - Stocks, Futures, Commodities…?"

Well, with the right attitude and dedication there is money to be made in every market.

However, there is one market that is still largely neglected by smaller traders even though it offers great profit potential and numerous trading opportunities. It is Forex or Foreign Exchange market. Why should you trade forex market?

Simply said, no other trading instrument comes even close to forex market when it comes to liquidity, 24hr market environment and last but not the least, profit potential. Forex (currency) market is the largest (most liquid) financial market in the world, with an average daily volume of more than US$ 1.5 trillion, which is more than all of the global equity markets combined.

Forex trading day starts in Wellington, New Zealand followed by Sydney, Australia, Hong Kong and Singapore. Three hours later trading day begins in Dubai (UAE) and other Middle Eastern countries. In couple of hours they are followed by Frankfurt, Zurich, Paris, Rome… London is the last one to open in Europe and five hours later it is followed by New York, Chicago and finally the West Coast.

The busiest hours are early European mornings because at that time major Asian exchanges are still open and European afternoons because at that time major US markets are open at the same time as Europe. Therefore, wherever you live and whatever your work hours are you can always find some time to participate in forex trading as opposed to stock market where you are usually limited to the regular business hours.

And when it comes to profit potential lets have a look at figures below:

Figure 1. is a daily candlestick chart for America Online (AOL) covering a period from June to September 2003. Figure 2. is a daily candlestick chart for S&P 500 e-mini contract (ES) covering a period from June to September 2003. Figure 3. is a daily candlestick chart for EUR/USD covering the same period.

We will now illustrate the difference in profit potential among those three popular trading instruments. Let's assume that in all three cases our start up capital is $5,000. We will choose the best five trades that we could have placed in each trading instrument (those trades are described with T1 ..T5 arrows on each chart) during the above mentioned four month period.

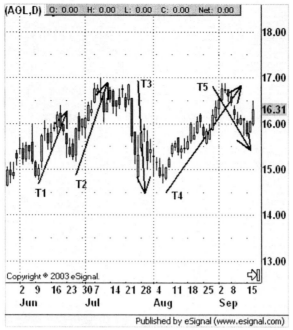

Figure 1.

As we have mentioned above we will assume a $5,000 start up capital and usual 2:1 equity trading margin.

$5,000 at 2:1 margin means with $5000 we can buy $10000 worth of stocks
T1 (trade 1) we can buy 650 shares of AOL at $15
15 – 16 = $1 per share * 650 shares = $650 profit
Now we have $5650 and we can buy 11300 worth of stocks
T2 (trade 2) we can buy 740 shares at $15.25
15.25-16.75 = 1.5 = $1110 profit
Now we have $6760 and we can buy $13,520 worth of stocks.
T3 (trade 3) we can short sell 800 shares at $16.75
16.75-15 = 1.75 * 800 = $1400 profit
Now we have $8160 and we can buy $16320 worth of stocks.
T4 (trade 4) we can buy 1000 shares at $15 per share
15 – 16.5 = 1.5 * 1000 = $1500 profit
Now we have $9660 and we can buy $19320 worth of stocks
T5 (trade 5) we can short sell 1200 shares at 16.75
16.75-16 = 0.75*1200 = $900

Total $10,560
Profit $5, 560 or 111%

Figure 2.

Again, we will assume $5,000 start up capital and current S&P 500 e-mini trading margin.

ES (Emini S&P)
$5,000 buys one contract at $3,600 margin
1 point = $0.5
T1 (trade 1) 95000 – 100500= 5500 * 0.5 = $2,750
$7,750 buys two contracts
T2 (trade 2) 100500- 97500 =3000*2*0.5 = $3,000
$10,750 buys two contracts
T3 (trade 3) 97500-100500 = 3000*2*0.5 = $3,000
$13750 buys three contracts
T4 (trade 4) 99000 –97000 = 2000*3*0.5 = $3,000
$16,750 buys four contracts
T5 (trade 5) 97000 – 102000 = 5000*4*0.5 $10,000

Total $26,750
Profit $21,750 or 435%

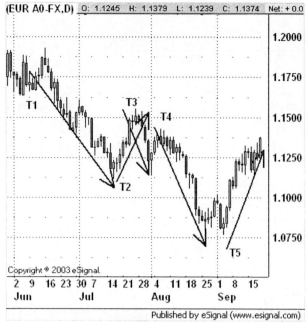

Figure 3.

We will again assume $5,000 start up capital and we will start with 1:20 margin, however we will slowly reduce our margin in order to minimize our risk exposure.

EUR/USD
$5,000 controlling $100,000 margin 1:20
T1 (trade 1) 1.185 – 1.110 = 7.5 cents profit = $7,500 profit
$12,500 controlling $200,000 margin 1:16
T2 (trade 2) 1.115 – 1.15 = 3.5 cents profit = $7,000 profit
$19,500 controlling $300,000 margin 1:15
T3 (trade 3) 1.15 – 1.125 = 2.5 cents profit = $7,500
$27,000 controlling $400,000 margin 1:15
T4 (trade 4) 1.13 – 1.09 = 4 cents profit = $16,000
$43,000 controlling $600,000 margin 1:14
T5 (trade 5) 1.08 – 1.13 = 5 cents = $30,000

Total $73,000
Profit $68,000 or 1,360%

From the examples above we can observe that currency trading offers at least 10 times more profit potential than a volatile tech stocks and at least double profit potential than S&P 500 e-mini contract when starting with the same start up capital.

We should also note that I did not cheat when choosing the above examples; no matter which multi day/month period you choose, currency trading will provide you with more opportunities, longer lasting trends and much better profit potential than any other trading instrument.

Many beginning traders don't fully understand the concept of leverage. Leverage can be your best friend and your worst enemy at the same time.

If you have a start up capital of $5,000 and if you trade on 1:50 margin, you can control $250,000 with your capital. However, a two percent move against you and your capital is completely wiped out. If you are a beginning trader you should not use more than 1:10 margin until you get comfortable and profitable and then and only then you can attempt to use higher margins up to 1:20. What does 1:10 margin mean? It means that with your $5,000 you will control $50,000.

Let's say you are trading EUR/USD and by using an entry strategy you have decided to enter the trade on a long side. That means that you are betting that USD will depreciate against EURO. Let's say current EUR/USD rate is 1.1584. Again, if your trading capital is $5,000 and you are using 1:10 leverage you will effectively be exchanging $50,000 to Euros. If the current rate is 1.1584 you will receive 50,000/1/1584 = 43,163 Euros.

If the trade goes in your direction that margin will work in your favor and 1% decline in USD will mean 10% increase in your start up capital. So if EUR/USD rate moves from 1.1584 to 1.1699, you will be able to exchange back your 43,163 Euros * 1.1699 to approximately $50,500 for a profit of $500. Since your start up capital was $5,000 it is effectively a 10% increase in your account. However, if the trade went against you and USD dollar appreciated 1% vs. EURO your account would be reduced to $4,500. You can then imagine what would have happened to your account if you were trading with 1:50 margin.

If you are trading currency futures it works in the same way although the minimum amount that you can buy is one contract. For example Canadian Dollar contract size is $100,000, Swiss Franc contract size is 125,000 SF, Euro Currency contract size is 125,000 EURO, E-mini Euro contract is 62,500 Euros. Initial margin requirement to purchase 1 E-mini Euro contract is $1,215. So with $1,215 you are controlling approximately $70,000. That is approximately 1:50 margin, however by having additional $5,000 in your account your margin will effectively be 1:10.

Another question that is often asked by aspiring traders is "What kind of trading approach should I use – day trading, swing trading, position trading? How many indicators should I use? Should I follow the TV news channels?..."

If you are facing similar dilemmas let me try to make an analogy. If you were attacked in a dark alley and you felt that your life was in real danger what kind of defense technique would you attempt to use. Would you attempt to kick your assailant with some fancy kung fu move that you saw in a movie? Or would you use some basic but brutally effective "knee to the groin", "thumb to the eye"

technique that is easy to implement and that you are 100% certain will have an effect?

When you have your hard earned money riding on your trades maybe your life is not at stake but your and your family's livelihood is. The goal of all the other traders in the market is to take your money. And if you are going to play around with some fancy tools and indicators that you don't even understand you can be assured that your hard earned money will be paying someone's BMW lease payments.

Forex market is a market where trends are long lasting, usually weeks and months at a time and are usually driven by technical analysis and that's why for the beginning trader the only viable strategy is to swing and position trade in attempt to catch those large multiday/week currency moves.

On the other hand intraday moves are mostly driven by news stories and economic reports, therefore day trading the forex market is something that a beginning trader should not do. For example there are 8 different reports due out in a single day, there is much news on a political front and at the same time you are following 10 different TA indicators. Are you seriously thinking that you can meaningfully digest all of that info?

Do you think that Warren Buffet listens to all that noise? If Jesse Livermore was still around do you think that he would be basing his trading decisions on CNBC commentaries?

To illustrate the difference between intraday and multiday/week forex trading lets have a look at Figures 4 and 5.

Figure 4.

Figure 5.

Figure 4. is a daily candlestick chart covering EUR/USD for an eight month period. As we can observe from the chart trends are long lasting and when the price crosses 20 day Moving Average it usually stays there for long periods of time.

On the other hand Figure 5. represents hourly candlestick chart covering EUR/USD for a seven day period. As we can observe from the chart there are no well defined trends, intraday moves are sudden, violent and brutal and they are usually driven by news, reports and even worse – rumors.

Now that we have decided that we will be trading looking for multiday/week currency trends we will define a simple and effective trading strategy that any beginner can understand and implement in a short period of time. In order to do so we will combine a few basic, hard core fundamental TA tools together with our own common sense.

Our example will deal with EUR/USD however if you live in Canada I would encourage you to trade USD/CAD, if you live in Australia you should trade USD/AUD, if you live in East Asia you should trade USD/JPY, if you live in UK you should trade either USD/GBP or EUR/GBP, if you live in European Union you are best off trading EUR/USD and finally if you live in the United States you should trade USD against the currency that you are most familiar with (EUR, JPY, GBP, CAD, SFR).

Trading the currency that you are familiar with has lots of advantages vs. trading currencies that you have never used.

For example a person who lives in Canada remembers approximate range of CAD vs. USD during past ten years or more and has much better understanding of those currencies than average person from Japan. Principles that are explained in this strategy can be used to trade any of the above currencies.

Although forex markets are in essence 24-hour markets, for the purpose of our strategy we will define when does the trading day start and when does it end. Let's have a look at figures below:

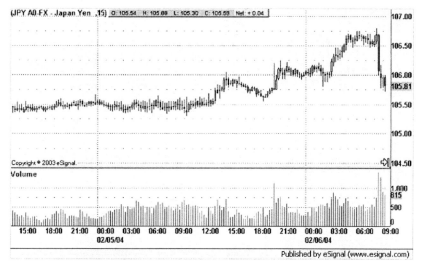

Figure 6.

Figure 7

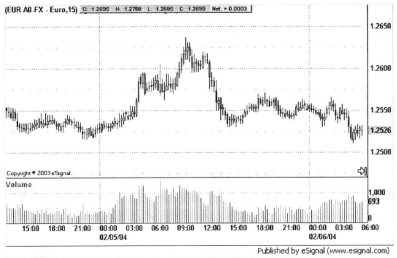

Figure 8.

Figures 6, 7 and 8 are 15-min candlestick charts for USD/JPY, USD/CAD and EUR/USD respectively. What do they all have in common? We can observe that the time of the lowest trading volume for all of them is at approximately 5pm EST or 10pm GMT. That is the time when almost all of the forex trading centers around the world are closed.

Therefore we will use 10pm GMT as the time when previous trading day ends and the new trading day begins. Here is an example: "You live in Europe. It is Thursday morning 9amGMT. Previous trading day has started on Tuesday 10pmGMT and it has ended Wednesday 10pmGMT. Another example: You live in North America. It is Thursday morning 9amEST. Previous trading day has started on Tuesday 5pm EST and it has ended Wednesday 5pm EST."

For those who don't know: Eastern Standard Time (EST) = Greenwich Mean Time (GMT) – 5

Why it is important to determine when does the trading day start and when does it end?

It is important because our strategy will be based on 3 day Pivot Points and in order to calculate 3 day Pivots we will need to combine 3 trading days into a single period.

You may be asking why aren't we using a single day pivot points and the answer is that our particular approach will attempt to catch larger multiday/week moves and 3 day Pivots will be better at eliminating much of the intraday noise.

How to calculate 3 day pivots?

Figure 9.

Figure 9 is a 15 minute bar chart covering a three day period for EUR/USD. From the chart we can observe values for the 3 Day High, 3 Day Low and 3 Day Close. From those values we will calculate pivot values. In our example those are the values covering period from Feb/2/2004 to Feb/4/2004.

Those are the values that we would use if we were to trade on Feb/5/2004. If we were to trade on Feb/6/2004 we would then calculate pivot values for the period Feb/3/2004 to Feb/5/2004.

We will use classic formula to calculate pivot values.

PP = (High + Low + Close)/3
Support = 2*PP – High
Resistance = 2*PP – Low

In our example:

3 Day High = 1.26
3 Day Low = 1.2388
3 Day Close = 1.254

PP = (1.26 + 1.2388 + 1.254)/3 = 1.251
Support = 2*1.251 – 1.26 = 1.242
Resistance = 2*1.251 – 1.2388 = 1.263

From these calculations we are interested in just two values.

We will compare the value of Resistance and 3 Day High and choose higher value.

In our example it is Resistance 1.263 (we will call it Upper Band)
We will compare the value of Support and 3 Day Low and choose lower value.
In our example it 3 Day Low 1.2388 (we will call it Lower Band)

Our next step will be to determine current trend.

We will do so by observing 20 Day Moving Average. If the current price is above 20 Day Moving Average we will adopt bullish approach. If the current price is below 20 Day Moving Average we will adopt bearish approach.

Our strategy is as follows:

If price above 20 Day MA then bullish. If bullish we will be looking to enter the trade only on the long side.

Our buy signals are:

➢ Price decidedly moving through the Upper Band on the way up.
➢ Price bouncing off the Lower Band and moving up.

If price is below the 20 Day MA then bearish. If bearish we will be looking to enter the trade only on a short side.

Our sell signals are.

➢ Price decidedly moving through the Lower Band on the way down.
➢ Price bouncing off the Upper Band and moving down.

Figure 10.

From the **Figure 10** we can observe that in our example the current price is below 20 Day Moving Average. Therefore we will adopt bearish approach.

We will then open a 10 min chart and draw those lines on it. We will also calculate the values for Second Level Support and Second Level Resistance

Support2 = PP – Resistance + Support
Resistance2 = PP – Support + Resistance

Support2 = 1.251 – 1.263 + 1.242 = 1.23
Resistance2 = 1.251 – 1.242 + 1.263 = 1.272

Figure 11.

By observing **Figure 11** we can note that our selling trading signal occurred at approximately 10am when the price bounced off the Upper Band.

Once we are in the trade and the price has started moving in our direction, we need to extract as much profit as possible. Not being able to do so will make you a losing trader in the long run.

How can a trader lose if he only takes small profits at a time? Profit is profit, isn't it? Not exactly… Profit of $550 is not the same as a profit of $850. If such profits are followed by three losses of $200 each, profit of $550 will become a $50 loss, while profit of $850 will become a $250 win. Do you get my point?

Profits are always followed by losses and if the profits are small they will not make up for the losses that will eventually and surely follow. However, becoming too greedy can turn a small profit into a loss. This will also make you lose money in the long run. The best solution to resolving these conflicts is to use trailing stops.

As the name says, trailing stop follows the price that is moving in your direction. For example let's say that we have entered a EUR/USD short trade at 1.264. We will automatically put our stop loss just above the resistance2.

The price starts to move in our direction and when it rises 0.5% we will sell one half of our position in order to protect some of our profits and we will move our stop loss up by using this formula:

CurrentStopLoss = PrevStopLoss + (PrevPrice - PrevStopLoss)*0.75 where CurrentStopLoss is calculated every time the price moves another 0.5% in the direction of our trade.

By selling one half of our position we made sure that our trade will make at least some profit and by letting other half of our position ride, we are making sure to be a part of any major move/trend that may follow.

Signpost Trading

By Michael Johnson www.three-bears.com

1. The Early Warning Signal – the 3dma.

I have been a futures player for many years. If you have the **Three Bears** trading plan you will know that one of the early *"smoothing"* signals and *early warning* movement change signals is the 3dma, the three day moving average. 3dma is a delayed indicator signal that takes a little of the kinkiness out of the market.

If you do not have the **Three Bears,** you need to work out the 3dma yourself. 3dma for my intents and purposes is always based on the close and is simple – as opposed to using *weighted* or *exponential* versions of dma.

Add the *"close"* for the last three days and divide your total by 3 (ignore decimal points and round **to the nearest whole number**).

Look at this market, which moves at the close from 3500 to 3555 and back to 3500 over 8 days.

	Close	3dma
Day 1	3500	
Day 2	3520	
Day 3	3530	3517 up
Day 4	3540	3530 up 30
Day 5	3555	3542 up 12
Day 6	**3540**	3545 up 03 but shrinking value
Day 7	3520	**3538** down 07
Day 8	3500	3520 down 18

Note the underlined 3540 does not change the 3dma until the next day. That's why this is called **a lagging indicator**.

This example does not show the high of the day or the low of the day.

The 3dma just takes a little of the zig-zag or "noise" as it is sometimes known, out of the share, index or commodity you are following.

The future I play is the SPI or The Share Price Index, and my entry point is the changeover from one direction to another on the 3dma. My early warning entry point.

The regular share market here in Australia closes at 4 PM. The SPI market closes at 4:30 PM and opens again at 5:10 PM for what is known as *the night market* when overseas influences from Europe – the Dax and the Ftse in particular, influence what may happen at the open the next day. Later in the evening and in the early morning, the US Market – the movement of the DOW (U S A Top 30 Stocks), and the S & P 500 (U S Top

500 stocks), which closely follows the DOW, have a large effect on our early trading positions.

So the changeover I look for, the 3dma, becomes evident to me when the regular share market has closed and if signals suit my entry point demands, I enter the market as soon as it opens for night trading at 5:10 PM.

Risk Management

There are many ways to manage the risk you are exposing yourself to using stop losses or take-profits.

I use the following basic formula.

I Buy at 3500 and having done so I would then issue the following instructions:

1. Sell at 3525.
2. Sell at 3480 on stop.
3. OCO GAM.

What I have done is take a Buy, expecting the market to go up. I have also locked in my profit at 25 points and have locked in my loss at 20 points.

OCO is One Cancels the Other, so if either of these Sell Points is reached, I will make a profit of 25 points or a loss of 20 points.

GAM is Good All Markets. That is both the day market and the night market, until one of the OCO positions is fulfilled and the other self cancels.

This index trades at $25 a point so
My profit would be 25 x 25 which is $625
My loss would be 20 x 25 which is $500
My brokerage is just over $50 being $25 in and $25 out.

Assume I am correct 7 times out of 10, wrong 2 times out of 10, break even 1 time in 10 when I change my *Sell instructions* and break even.

7 x 25 = 175 points
2 x 20 = 40 points
1 x 00 = 00 points
Summing up 175 points – 40 points = 135 points x $25 = $3375.00

Let's assume I am trading really badly in a flat market (highly unlikely).

I am right only 6 times out of 10 (This never happens – I do better than this).

6 x 25 = 150 points = $3750
Less 4 x 20 = 80 = $2000. = $1750 profit.

That's probably the worst possible scenario in a totally flat market.

Here's what I've found and I've been playing this method for 5 years now.
Through many ups and downs, many bull markets, and many bear markets.
But all I am really concerned about is the short term trading that is about to happen.

There are two ways to play it:

If the Market is Bullish:
I mean, if the market is very bullish, I would assume that the retracement was short and sharp. I would possibly not play the 3dma when it came up as a down arrow (i.e., a change to downwards). After all, it had already taken 3 days to achieve this and it may not have another 25 points left in the downward run.

Right now I am assuming that the only indicator I have is the 3dma.
Later on I will show you how to refine this with a market direction indicator that keeps you away from the bad trades.

I would wait until the next "WITH THE TREND" bullish up arrow or *turn around* came up, and then play the market upwards. This way I would be right 9 times out of 10.

We all know "the trend is your friend." So don't go against it.

However, quite often there is a 25 points downward movement to be taken, - sometimes more - and if there was no big change overnight, I can step in and change my orders; i.e., stop loss and stop profit at any time I wish to take a smaller stop loss. In other words, although I do have a stop profit and a stop loss in place, the trade is live and I have the ability to stop a trade at any time it looks to be doubtful. I can keep a trade going if it looks bigger than expected.

Here's a hint:
Often when playing against the trend, the share will show a spike for the day. If you don't have a stop profit in place you'll miss cashing in on that spike. This often reflects a change in *support* or *resistance* that can totally reverse a market in minutes.

If I suspect a long trade and haven't hit my 25 point stop profit, I can cancel my stop profit and use a trailing stop in line WITH THE TREND MOVEMENTS.

If you want a real simple plan, a KISS plan with no emotion to be involved, play the 20 Point stop loss 25 point stop profit every time.

If you want to increase your strike rate, go to your technical analysis and make sure you understand the trend (or see my slow stochastic second opinion below). And play only those trades that are resuming as "WITH THE TREND" trades.

If the market is going with you and you do not take a stop profit in the first trading day after you enter a trade, renegotiate your stop loss position with your broker. Take the "trailing stop loss" position, adjustable every day until you are stopped out at a much bigger profit than your preliminary 25 points of course.

Remember, you can trade futures either way - Bullish or Bearish.

If the Market is Bearish:
If the market is bearish and the 3dma has suddenly changed to downwards, I would reverse the procedure outlined above. **Sell first** and **Buy later,** with the same stop losses as *"Buy at"*, of course.

For example:
Index 3500. I Sell at 3500.
My order to my broker is
Buy 3475. Buy 3520 on stop.
One cancels the other.
Good All Markets.

This is my Sell procedure and it is exactly the same as my Buy procedure, but in reverse.

The market goes down 25 points and my collect order Buys for my 25 points profit.

If the market has reversed a full 20 points (unusual on the night market), I would have lost 20 points in total as the Good All Markets would have been my effective exit strategy.

I know there are many players who have to go to work and this would be the perfect strategy for them because you can play the short term and you don't have the pressure of having to follow the markets. There is also no worry or stress of not knowing what will happen. The worst that can happen is you lose 20 points. The best that can happen is you profit by 25 points.

You place **your entry price** and **your exit strategy** all in one call, and let the market look after you from that point on… remembering that *"The market is always right."*

This is as near to a perfect mechanical system as I can create. But it is also an excellent "manually watched system" if you prefer, and frankly I do. Because I can use a trailing stop loss. Which if you are not a market watcher, you can place every night when you check up your position.

Remember KISS. Keep It Simple Sir. And never ever fail to have an exit position in place. This may or may not include your stop-profit, but it must always include a stop loss.

In the following chart, you'll find the SPI Index for the last 30 days at the time it was written:

Date	Open	High	Low	Close	3dma	Points	
29/03/04	3439	3439	3419	3419	3416 ↓		
30/03/04	3435	3438	3422 ☐	**3425**	3420 ☐	T1	+ 25
31/03/04	3435	3436 ☐	3418	3419	3421 ☐		
01/04/04	3420	3462	3420	3458	3434 ☐		
02/04/04	3467	3467	3446 ☐	3450	3442 ☐		
05/04/04	3463	3478	3450 ☐	3477	3461 ☐		
06/04/04	3481	**3486**	3465 ☐	3466	3464 ☐	**61 pts.**	
07/04/04	3473	3484	3460	3466	3469 ☐		
08/04/04	3461	3468 ☐	3453	**3454**	3462 ☐	T2	+ 25
09/04/04	GOOD	FRIDAY					
12/04/04	EASTER	MONDAY					
13/04/04	3461	3472	3441	3455	3458 ☐		
14/04/04	3439	3455	3433	3453	3454 ☐		
15/04/04	3448	3455	3419	3422	3443 ☐		
16/04/04	3432	3438	**3412**	3437	3437 ☐	**42 pts.**	
19/04/04	3443	3444	3429	3443	3434 ☐		
20/04/04	3443	3467	3441 ☐	**3464**	3448 ☐	T3	- 20
21/04/04	3455	3458	3445 ☐	3447	3451 ☐		
22/04/04	3455	**3461**	3436	3442	3451	**- 3 pts.**	
23/04/04	3458	3477	3458	**3461**	3450 ☐	T4	+ 1
26/04/04	3461	3469	**3456**	**3460**	3454 ☐	**5 pts.** T5	
27/04/04	3457	**3460** ☐	3444	3456	3459 ☐	**0 pts.**	- 4
28/04/04	3456	3464	3445	**3445**	3453 ☐	T6	+ 25
29/04/04	3419	3421	**3387**	3394	3431 ☐	**58 pts.**	

Here's a virtual calendar month in a very flat market with a breakout only at the end.

I've marked the trades on the basis that you are taking the **automatic entry** on the 3dma change.

You have a 20 point stop loss and a 25 point stop profit.

On the event that a trade is unfulfilled and the 3dma changes again, **you exit one trade** and **take the opposite one** at the same time, like T4 and T5.

6 Trades, marked T1 to T6. The market is flat, but three trades were successful and three were mediocre.

Entry Points are **change of 3dma direction.**

Exit Points are + 24 or – 20 or new changeover of direction.

T1 Max points available were 61 but we took an easy + 25.
T2 Max points available were 42 but we took an easy + 25
T3 We got stopped out on Max - 20
T4There were 5 point in it but we took the direction change over for +1
T5 No gain and at direction change we lost 4 points -4
T6 Max points available were 58 points but we took an easy + 25

The total for this month with a single contract played, we had:
Pluses 76 minuses 24 = 51 points in our favor x $25 = $1275.00
If your broker's fee is $300, you made $975.00 which is not bad for a quiet sideways month.

Here's the SPI Chart for the same period (Notice it was a pretty flat market):

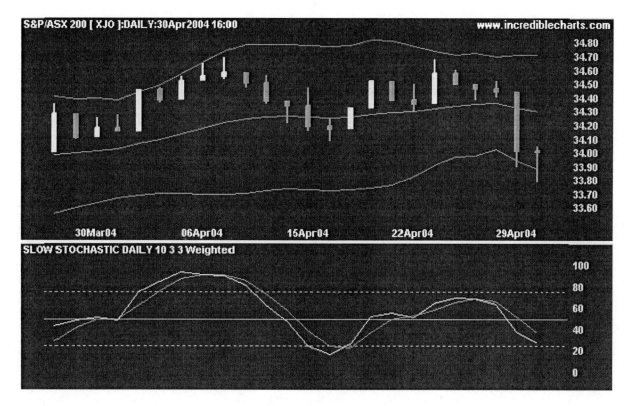

KISS Confirmation. - Your Second Opinion.

This is where we get smart and add **a second opinion** that confirms or denies us the opinion we need to take a trade. Of course you can take them the way I outlined, but by using **slow stochastic** ss here you are asking for the "trend" as indicated by ss.

First, you'll see I've put in the **Slow Stochastic** under the chart.

I'm now going to lead you to a site where you can set up your S&P 500 or ASX 200, the XJO or whatever, and then place the slow stochastic below it :

The site is www.incrediblecharts.com

When you open the slow stochastic under "indicators" the parameters to set your slow stochastic to will be in the center of the page.

Here's how to set this up.

1. Daily. OK.
2. .%K - **change to "10"**
3. %K slowing leave at 3
4. %D leave at 3
5. **Change set type of indicator to "weighted"**
6. **Overbought change to "75"**
7. **Oversold change to "25"**

Slow stochastic:
1. If the green line is above the red the trend is upwards.
2. If the green line is below the red the trend is downwards.

Many people believe that where the green crosses the red is a buy or sell signal. Others believe the oversold/overbought areas are the most suitable for using this indicator.

Look at what happens when we look at the 6 Trading Points of the 3dma and seek to see if the slow stochastic set as above confirms the 3dma. If the 3dma is up and the ss is in **buy mode,** the future can be taken. If the 3dma is down and the ss is in **sell mode** the future can be taken. If they disagree with each other the trade should not be taken.

Trade	Date	3dma	Slow Stoch	Success
T1	March 3rd	Up	Up	+ 25 points
T2	April 4th	Down	Down	+ 25 points
T3	April 20th	Up	Down	No trade
T4	April 23rd	Down	Up	No Trade
T5	April 23rd	Up	Up	- 4 points

T6   April 28th   Down Down   + 25 points

Total on a single contract + 75 points – 4 points = 71 points = $1775 dollars
$200 for your broker, gives you $1575.00 for a quiet month.

I submitted the following request to my friend Joe who plays this method on several indices around the world and I asked him to check out the same dates for the S&P as I had outlined for the SPI here in Australia.

Joe pointed out that it was **the flattest month he had come across** for a while and that the market did not go into downward breakout until the end of the month.

Here is how he outlined the trades he uses:
 www.incrediblecharts.com

Joe told me he was always home before the market closed and he took the trade "on the close" or just before it, and had the 3dma and the charting position all worked out long before the closing bell. He had his trades placed electronically to coincide with the close.

But he did not take the Easter weekend trade which he includes for completeness.

On the following page is the S&P 500 INDEX (SPX), a flat market going nowhere.

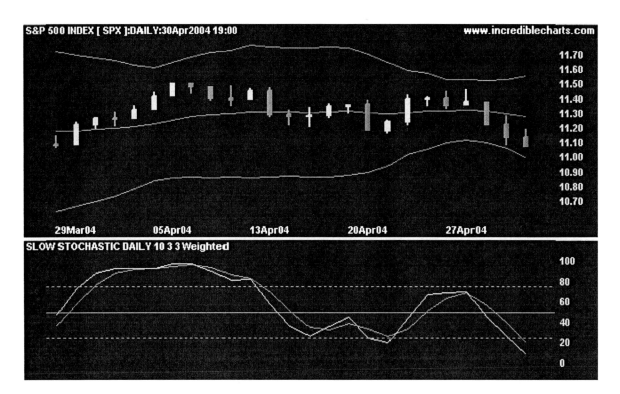

Date	Open	High	Low	Close	3dma		Points	
29/03/04	1108	1124	1108	**1122**	1113	↑	T1	
30/03/04	1122	1127	1119	1127	1119	⊔		
31/03/04	1127	1130	1121	1126	1125	⊔		
01/04/04	1126	1135	1126	1132	1128	⊔		
02/04/04	1132	1144	1132	1141	1133	⊔		
05/04/04	1141	**1150**	1141	1150	1141	⊔		
06/04/04	1150	1150	1143	1148	1146	⊔		
07/04/04	1148	1148	1138	1140	1146	⊔		
08/04/04	1140	1149	1134	**1139**	1142	↓	T2	
09/04/04	Good	Friday						
12/04/04	1139	1147	1139	1145	1141	⊔		
13/04/04	1145	1147	1127	1129	1137	⊔		
14/04/04	1129	1132	1122	1128	1134	⊔		
15/04/03	1128	1134	**1120**	1128	1128	⊔		
16/04/04	1128	1136	1126	**1134**	1130	↑	T3	
19/04/04	1134	1136	1129	1135	1132	⊔		
20/04/04	1135	**1139**	1118	**1118**	1129	⊔	T4	
21/04/04	1118	1125	1116	1124	1125	⊔		
22/04/04	1124	1142	1122	**1139**	1127	↑	T5	
23/04/04	1139	1141	1134	1140	1134	⊔		
26/04/04	1140	1145	1132	1135	1138	⊔		
27/04/04	1135	**1146**	1135	**1138**	1137	⊔	T6	
28/04/04	1138	1138	1121	1122	1131	⊔		
29/04/04	1122	1128 ⊔	**1108**	1113	1124	⊔		

T1. March 29th - Up trade: This was an up-run from previous day and I stayed with it for 25 points. I didn't stop myself out as there were **continuous higher lows.**

T2. April 8th - Down trade: This shows a loss of 6 points as that was the close a day after taking the trade. However, this was a long weekend and this trade was not actually taken. So, the final month's profit is thus 6 points larger.

It is a sensible policy of many traders when working a trading market not to trade over a long weekend where lower volumes can often give a false position.

T3. April 16th - Up trade: After 1 day I was up a point so I hung in there. I stopped myself out at the close the next day for a loss of 16 points.

T4. April 20th - Down trade: I Took the 6 point loss at the close on the following day.

T5. April 22nd - Up market: Again, the market is flat and after two days, I stopped out for a loss of 4 points.

T6. April 27th - Down market: There was an easy 25 points profit on this one and the market kept on going. But after that flat market I did take the 25 points.

Summary: +25 –6 –16 –6 –4 +25 gives a total for the month of **plus 18**. Actually, on a month where few traders made any profit on the volatile swings of the daily ups and downs, to come out ahead was a great triumph.

Note Joe's entry times and also note how he checks out the higher bottoms as a rising market sign and lower tops as a falling market sign. If such signs appear he stops himself out without waiting for the 20 points.

In closing, remember that whatever technical analysis indicates whatever stop losses or stop profits you activate:

The market is always right!

SilverPlatterStocks™ Trading Strategy

By Robert DiMattia www.silverplatterstocks.com

The Buying/Selling Process for SilverPlatterStocks™ is based on these 5 concepts:

1.)   Entry Time Categories
2.)   RBI (Range Break-out Index)
3.)   Chart Patterns
4.)   Exit Signals
5.)   Volume

Entry Time Categories

The first Entry Time Category is called the "Open Entry."

This is the name of the pattern where the price will open with little or no gap and then rise after the open.

Stocks within this entry time are bought right after the market opens at a time frame between 9:30 am ET and 15 minutes after the particular stock opens.

How does the trader know if a stock is an Open Entry stock candidate?

The Open Price must be at or below a given point in relation to the stock's previous day's closing price. This point is the Open Entry Price.

The trader is given the Open Entry Price for each stock pick on the SilverPlatterStocks™ Selection Form.

IF THE STOCK OPENS *AT OR BELOW* THE OPEN ENTRY STOCK PRICE, IT IS AN OPEN ENTRY STOCK.

The second Entry Time Category is called the "Bounce."

This is the name of the pattern where the price will gap at the open, and then drop down to or below a given point, and then retrace back up.

This pattern is named "Bounce" because the buy takes place after the bounce from this bottom point.

The bottom point limit the price must hit or pass on its downward movement is called "Bounce Bottom Point." The actual bottom price the stock hits is called the "Bounce Bottom Price."

Stocks within this entry time are bought between 9:50 am ET and 10:20 am ET after the pronounced downturn.

How does the trader know if a stock is a Bounce stock candidate?

The Open Price must be at or above a given point in relation to the stock's previous close. This point is the Bounce Price.

The trader is given the Bounce Price for each stock pick on the SilverPlatterStocks™ Selection Form.

IF THE STOCK OPENS *AT OR ABOVE* THE BOUNCE PRICE, IT IS A BOUNCE STOCK.

Note: the Bounce Price for any given stock is always higher than the Open Entry Price. Therefore no stock can be both. Every stock that is bought will be either an Open Entry stock or a Bounce stock.

What if a stock opens below the Bounce Stock Price and above the Open Entry Stock?

That stock is called a "No Man's Land." That won't happen often, but when it does the trader should **pass on the stock** unless the price rises to or above a given point and then retraces. (This is called a P-Bounce and is covered below.)

Therefore, as soon as the Open Price is determined for a given stock, the trader knows if the stock is an Open Entry or a Bounce stock.

RBI

RBI stands for Range Break-out Index. Every stock has one for any given trading day.

The trader is given the RBI for each stock pick on the SilverPlatterStocks™ Selection Form.

The RBI is simply how many points the stock must rise on an upswing to reach the buy point. It is also how many points the stock must fall on a down turn to reach the sell point.

The whole idea of RBI is the trader needs to be sure that the stock is making its up move (as opposed to experiencing its normal range movement) before buying, and that it's making its down move (as opposed to experiencing its normal range movement) before selling.

Chart Patterns

As discussed above, there are two Entry Time Categories.

There are two chart patterns for *each* Entry Time Category.

The two chart patterns for any Open Entry Stock:

#1) "Up and Away"

This is the fastest to buy, and in many cases the fastest to sell and the most profitable pattern.

Upon market opening at 9:30 am ET (as soon as the specific stock opens) the trader notes the Open Price of the stock onto the SilverPlatterStocks™ Selection Form.

At that instant, the Selection Form will indicate if the stock is an Open Entry Stock and provide the "Up & Away" Buy Price if it is.

If the stock is an Open Entry stock, the trader must get ready. At this point the trader should allow 20 or 30 seconds to pass to allow the price direction to be established.

If the price moves up by the RBI amount (to the Buy Price provided by the SilverPlatterStocks™ Selection Form), the trader buys.

#2) "V and Up"

This is a variation of the "Up and Away." One of two things will happen in this entry pattern:

a.) The stock will open with the upward movement as above, but before it hits the RBI, it will turn around. It will hit a point at its bottom and turn around again and move right back up so the chart looks like a "V."

b.) The stock will go right down from the open, hit a point at its bottom and turn around back up so the chart also looks like a "V."

In either case above the trader notes the price point of the stock at the bottom of this "V" onto the SilverPlatterStocks™ Selection Form. At that instant, the Selection Form will provide the "V & Up" Buy Price.

With each stock pick the SilverPlatterStocks™ Selection Form will provide the "V-RBI" which is usually a penny more than the regular RBI.

When the stock subsequently moves up by an amount equal to the "V-RBI" (to the "V & Up" Buy Price given by the SilverPlatterStocks™ Selection Form), the trader buys.

What if the stock doesn't hit the V-RBI?

THE TRADER MUST PASS ON THE STOCK.

What if the stock makes more than one "V" before hitting the V-RBI?

THE TRADER MUST PASS ON THE STOCK.

For either the "Up and Away", or the "V and Up", if the upward movement is not pronounced, and the stock starts ranging sideways before hitting the RBI, THE TRADER MUST PASS ON THE STOCK.

If 15 minutes have passed from the time the stock has opened and the RBI hasn't been hit, THE TRADER MUST PASS ON THE STOCK.

<u>The two chart patterns for any Bounce Entry Stock:</u>

<u>#1) "Bounce"</u>

Upon market opening at 9:30 am ET (as soon as the specific stock opens) the trader notes the Open Price of the stock on the SilverPlatterStocks™ Selection Form.

At that instant, the Selection Form will indicate if the stock is a Bounce Stock and provide the Bounce Bottom Point if it is.

If the stock is a Bounce Stock there will not be a buy until 9:50 am ET at the earliest.

The chart pattern that must appear for any Bounce stock is a dramatic drop in the price between the Open Price and the Buy-Window. (Remember, the Buy-Window is from 9:50 am ET to 10:20 am ET.)

The stock must fall *to or below* the Bounce Bottom Point within the Buy-Window.

Specific market forces shorting this stock are what cause this drop. There can be up turns (false bottoms) along this drop. That's fine as long as the price reaches or crosses below the Bounce Bottom Point between 9:50 am ET and 10:20 am ET

With the above conditions met, the trader must watch for the stock price to move up from the Bounce Bottom. When it does, the trader buys as soon as the price hits the RBI.

As soon as the trader enters the actual Bounce Bottom Price onto the SilverPlatterStocks™ Selection Form, the Buy Price is provided by the Selection Form.

For example: The Bounce Price for a stock is given on the SPS Selection Form to be 25.50.

The Bounce Bottom Point for the same stock is given to be 24.75. The RBI is given to be .06

The stock opens after the first-minute tick at 25.55. (Since it is at or above 25.50, it's a go so far.)

The stock price makes a dip with one or two false-bottoms along the way and hits bottom at 24.60 at 10:05 am ET. (Since that is at or below the Bounce Bottom Point of 24.75, and within the Buy-Window time range, it's still a go.)

That 24.60 Bounce Bottom Price is entered into the Selection Form and the Buy Price of 24.66 is provided by the form.

The stock price starts its rise from the Bounce Bottom Price of 24.60. The trader buys when the price hits 24.66 (.06 RBI).

#2) "P-Bounce"

This is a slight variation of the Bounce stock.

In a P-Bounce stock the price rises before making its drop to the Bounce Bottom. This rise in price *pulls up* the Bounce Bottom Point. The name P-Bounce is short for Pull-Bounce.

There are two types of stocks that become P-Bounces:

A.) It can be a stock that opens in "No-Man's Land."

(Recall that No-Man's Land is the designation of any stock with an Open Price higher than the Open Entry Price and lower the Bounce Price.

Also recall that the Open Entry Price and the Bounce Price are provided on the SPS Selection Form.)

As stated above, a stock that opens in No-Man's Land can become a P-Bounce if the price rises after the open to or above the Bounce Price.

For example:

The Bounce Price for a stock is given to be 25.50.

The Open Entry Price for the same stock is given to be 24.40

The stock opens at 24.75. (Since this is above 24.40 and below 25.50, it's No-Man's Land so far.)

The price goes up to 25.50 before it makes its dip to the Bounce Bottom.

Since the rise before the dip peaked at or above the 25.50 Bounce Price, this is a P-Bounce candidate.

> B.) It can be a stock that opens as a Bounce stock (that is higher than the Bounce Price that is provided on the **SPS** Selection Form with each pick).

It becomes a P-Bounce if the price rises before making its drop to the Bounce Bottom Point. When this happens the trader enters the highest price point before the drop onto the **SPS** Selection Form and the Selection Form will instantly provide a new higher Bounce Bottom Point.

Exit Signals

The trader will sell all SilverPlatterStocks™ when one of four things occurs:

> 1.) The stock price passes the Target Sell Price, hits a peak, and then makes a subsequent price drop by the RBI amount. (The Target Sell Price is provided on the **SPS** Selection Form with each stock.)

> 2.) The stock price passes the Target Sell Price, hits a peak, and then hits the Target Sell Price on the subsequent price drop. (The Target Sell Price is provided on the **SPS** Selection Form with each stock.)

> 3.) The stock price hits the Stop-Loss Price. (This is also provided on the **SPS** Selection Form with each stock.)

> 4.) The stock times-out at 11:00 am ET. If #1), #2) or #3) above haven't hit, and the stock price is ranging sideways or moving down, it is usually best to sell at whatever the in-between price is at 11:00 am ET.
>
> > **EXCEPTION TO THIS:** The trader should not sell at 11:00 am ET if the stock price is going up regardless if the Target Sell Price has been hit or not. The trader should never sell a stock that's going up until 3:45 pm ET.

THE TRADER DOES NOT SELL AT THE TARGET PRICE WHEN IT IS HIT ON AN UPTURN.

A basic principle of all investing applies here: cut your losses and let your profits run.

The trader must hold on when the stock price hits and passes the Target Sell Price on the way up. The trader does not sell at the point the Target Sell Price is first hit.

The trader sells after the rising stock price has hit and passed the Target Sell Price, and then has made a subsequent downturn, when the *first* of these two things happen:

1.)   The stock hits the Target Sell Price again, this time on the way down.

2.)   The stock moves down from its peak the same number of points as its RBI. (The trader must always uses the RBI to sell; not the V-RBI even on a "V & UP.")

Note: if the stock price blasts upward past the Target Sell Price and does not hit #1) or #2) above on subsequent downturns, the trader just hangs in for the profitable ride to no later than 3:45 pm ET.

At all times the trader must sell at 3:45 pm ET (15 minutes before the market closes) no matter what the stock is doing at that point.

THE TRADER MUST NEVER, NEVER, NEVER HOLD ONTO A TRADE OVERNIGHT.

This overrides all other rules.

Volume

Each stock has its own volume, which is a measure of how heavily it is traded. This affects all SPS traders because when it is time to sell, we must be able to do so quickly.

This is accomplished if we have enough buyers at all times when we are in a trade. This, in turn, is accomplished if we analyze the volume for each stock and leave sufficient margin to insure there are buyers whenever we sell.

This is all done for the trader. With each SilverPlatterStock™ the trader is given the maximum number of shares to buy for that day's trade on the SilverPlatterStocks™ Selection Form.

He or she can buy less, but MUST NOT BUY MORE.

Included below are four actual trades which illustrate all of these 5 concepts.

Entry Time Categories
    2 actual Open Entry trades & 2 actual Bounce trades

RBI (Range Break-out Index)
    3 actual Open Entry trades with a 4 cent RBI & 1 with a 6 cent RBI

Chart Patterns
    1 actual trade for each of the 4 Chart Patterns

Exit Signals

All 4 actual trades where the Target Sell Price is passed, the price forms a Post-Target Peak and the Sell takes place on the subsequent RBI drop.

Volume

The volumes on these 4 actual trades range from $12,412 to $44,914

Depending on the amount you have available to invest, your total net profit for any given SilverPlatterStock™ trade is directly proportional to the volume limit for a SPS stock.

The trading data of the 5 categories from these four trades are listed on the first table.

The trading results from these four trades are listed on the second table.

DATE	STOCK SYMB	ENTRY TIME CATGRY	RBI (OR V-RBI)	CHART PATTERN	EXIT SIGNAL	VOLUME
12/4/2003	MBG	OPEN ENTRY	V-RBI: .05	V & UP	43.50 PEAK LESS RBI	$27,853
12/18/2003	ATVI	BOUNCE	RBI: .04	BOUNCE	18.40 PEAK LESS RBI	$23,889
1/13/2004	MHS	OPEN ENTRY	RBI: .04	UP & AWAY	35.93 PEAK LESS RBI	$44,994
2/24/2004	OPWV	BOUNCE	RBI: .06	P-BOUNCE	14.71 PEAK LESS RBI	$12,412

DATE	STOCK SYMBOL	BUY PRICE	SELL PRICE	BUY TIME	SELL TIME	GROSS PROFIT
12/4/2003	MBG	42.35	43.46	9:37 AM	9:55 AM	2.62%
12/18/2003	ATVI	17.73	18.36	9:50 AM	10:06 AM	3.55%
1/13/2004	MHS	34.76	35.89	9:37 AM	10:08 AM	3.25%
2/24/2004	OPWV	14.31	14.65	10:14 AM	10:43 AM	2.38%

The actual completed SilverPlatterStocks™ Selection Forms and the illustrated charts for these four trades are displayed on the next eight pages:

SilverPlatterStock Selection (Sample of V & Up Chart Pattern)	
Thursday December 04 2003	
Stock Symbol:	**MBG**
Stock Rating:	**85.5**
Previous Day Closing Price:	**42.72**
RBI:	**0.04**
V-RBI:	**0.05**
Type the Maximum $ Amount You Want to Invest:	$10,000
Volume Restricted Maximum $ Amount to Invest:	$27,853
Number of Shares You Will Buy:	236
'OPEN ENTRY' Price the Stock must open AT OR BELOW to qualify:	43.25
'BOUNCE' Price the Stock must open AT OR ABOVE to qualify:	43.57
Type Open Price Here (Eg 24.53) (SEE NOTE AT BOTTOM):	42.75
OPEN ENTRY; Keep Your Eye on Your Stock Chart for an Entry Signal	
If You Have a Trade, it Will Occur Anytime From Open to 15 Minutes Past Open	
'V & Up' Chart Pattern	
If Price Falls to 1 'V' Within 15 Min of Open, Type in 'V' Bottom Here:	42.30
If Price Rises From 'V' Bottom to 42.35, BUY. (Look at 'Ask' & 'Last'.)	**BUY: 42.35**
If a Bounce or P-Bounce, Type in the Actual Bounce Bottom Point:	
Type in Your Buy Price Here (Eg 25.67):	42.35
If This Stock is a Play, Target Sell Price (If Blank, Type Bounce Bottom Above):	**42.71**
.....And to Determine Your Stop-Loss Price:	**41.93**
Type in Your Sell Price Here (Eg 26.90):	43.46
.....To Determine Your Profit Percentage:	**2.62%**
IMPORTANT NOTE REGARDING OPEN PRICE:	
1) Wait for the 9:30 A.M. tick. 2) Then look for change in Ask,	
Bid & Last Prices. 3) At the Point You Have First Bid and Ask	
Movement & a Reasonable Bid & Ask Spread, and Volume,	
Mark the Corresponding Last Price as Your Open Price.	
(Set the Bottom of Your Graph to Show Volume.)	
The Stock Has NOT Opened if: 1.) There is No Trading	
Volume, or 2.) There is no Movement in the Bid and Ask,	

THURS 12/4/03 MBG

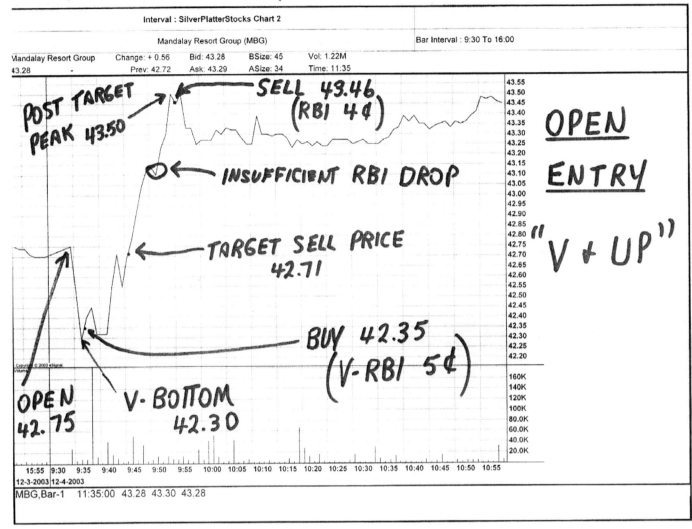

Interval : SilverPlatterStocks Chart 2

Mandalay Resort Group (MBG)

Bar Interval : 9:30 To 16:00

| Mandalay Resort Group | Change: + 0.56 | Bid: 43.28 | BSize: 45 | Vol: 1.22M |
| 43.28 | Prev: 42.72 | Ask: 43.29 | ASize: 34 | Time: 11:35 |

POST TARGET
PEAK 43.50

SELL 43.46
(RBI 4¢)

OPEN
ENTRY

"V + UP"

INSUFFICIENT RBI DROP

TARGET SELL PRICE
42.71

BUY 42.35
(V-RBI 5¢)

OPEN
42.75

V-BOTTOM
42.30

MBG, Bar-1 11:35:00 43.28 43.30 43.28

ENTRY TIME CATEGORY: Open Entry

RBI: V-RBI (on Buy) 5 cents; RBI (on Sell) 4 cents

CHART PATTERN: V & Up

EXIT SIGNAL: Post Target Peak of 43.50 Less RBI of .04 = Sell at 43.46

VOLUME: Purchase Maximum Limit: $27,853

SilverPlatterStock Selection (Sample of Bounce Chart Pattern)	
Thursday December 18 2003	
Stock Symbol:	**ATVI**
Stock Rating:	**86.0**
Previous Day Closing Price:	**16.41**
RBI:	**0.04**
V-RBI:	**0.05**
Type the Maximum $ Amount You Want to Invest:	**$10,000**
Volume Restricted Maximum $ Amount to Invest:	**$23,889**
Number of Shares You Will Buy:	**564**
'OPEN ENTRY' Price the Stock must open AT OR BELOW to qualify:	**16.62**
'BOUNCE' Price the Stock must open AT OR ABOVE to qualify:	**16.74**
Type Open Price Here (Eg 24.53) (SEE NOTE AT BOTTOM):	17.97
BOUNCE	
LOOK FOR AND ENTER HIGHEST P-BOUNCE PEAK PRICE	
A P-BOUNCE PEAK PRICE WILL PULL UP THE BOUNCE BOTTOM	
...If New, Higher Peak Price, Enter Here	
To Determine Your Bounce Bottom Upper Limit:	**17.76**
If a Bounce or P-Bounce, Type in the Actual Bounce Bottom Point:	17.69
Type in Your Buy Price Here (Eg 25.67):	17.73
If This Stock is a Play, Target Sell Price (If Blank, Type Bounce Bottom Above):	**17.88**
.....And to Determine Your Stop-Loss Price:	**17.55**
Type in Your Sell Price Here (Eg 26.90):	18.36
.....To Determine Your Profit Percentage:	**3.55%**

IMPORTANT NOTE REGARDING OPEN PRICE:
1) Wait for the 9:30 A.M. tick. 2) Then look for change in Ask,
Bid & Last Prices. 3) At the Point You Have First Bid and Ask
Movement & a Reasonable Bid & Ask Spread, and Volume,
Mark the Corresponding Last Price as Your Open Price.
(Set the Bottom of Your Graph to Show Volume.)
The Stock Has NOT Opened if: 1.) There is No Trading
Volume, or 2.) There is no Movement in the Bid and Ask,

THURSDAY 12/18/03 ATVI

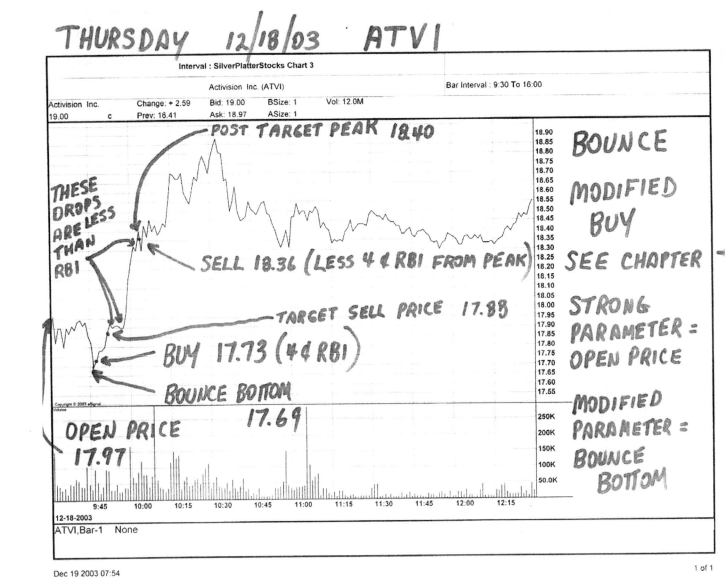

ENTRY TIME CATEGORY: Bounce

RBI: 4 cents

CHART PATTERN: Bounce

EXIT SIGNAL: Post Target Peak of 18.40 Less RBI of .04 = Sell at 18.36

VOLUME: Purchase Maximum Limit: $23,889

SilverPlatter Stock Selection (Sample of Up & Away Chart Pattern)	
Tuesday January 13 2004	
Stock Symbol:	MHS
Stock Rating:	86.5
Previous Day Closing Price:	34.40
RBI:	0.04
V-RBI:	0.05
Type the Maximum $ Amount You Want to Invest:	$10,000
Volume Restricted Maximum $ Amount to Invest:	$44,994
Number of Shares You Will Buy:	288
'OPEN ENTRY' Price the Stock must open AT OR BELOW to qualify:	34.83
'BOUNCE' Price the Stock must open AT OR ABOVE to qualify:	35.09
Type Open Price Here (Eg 24.53) (SEE NOTE AT BOTTOM):	34.72
OPEN ENTRY; Keep Your Eye on Your Stock Chart for an Entry Signal	
If You Have a Trade, it Must Occur Anytime From Open to 15 Minutes Past Open	
If Price Rises From Open to 34.76, BUY. (Look at 'Ask' & 'Last', See Chpt 2.) OR	
If Price Falls to 1 'V' Within 15 Min of Open, Type in 'V' Bottom Here:	
If Price Rises From 'V' Bottom by 'V-RBI', BUY. (Look at 'Ask' & 'Last'.)	
If a Bounce or P-Bounce, Type in the Actual Bounce Bottom Point:	
Type in Your Buy Price Here (Eg 25.67):	34.76
If This Stock is a Play, Target Sell Price (If Blank, Type Bounce Bottom Above):	35.06
.....And to Determine Your Stop-Loss Price:	34.41
Type in Your Sell Price Here (Eg 26.90):	35.89
.....To Determine Your Profit Percentage:	3.25%

IMPORTANT NOTE REGARDING OPEN PRICE:

1) Wait for the 9:30 A.M. tick. 2) Then look for change in Ask,
Bid & Last Prices. 3) At the Point You Have First Bid and Ask
Movement & a Reasonable Bid & Ask Spread, and Volume,
Mark the Corresponding Last Price as Your Open Price.
(Set the Bottom of Your Graph to Show Volume.)
The Stock Has NOT Opened if: 1.) There is No Trading
Volume, or 2.) There is no Movement in the Bid and Ask,

TUESDAY 1/13/04 MHS

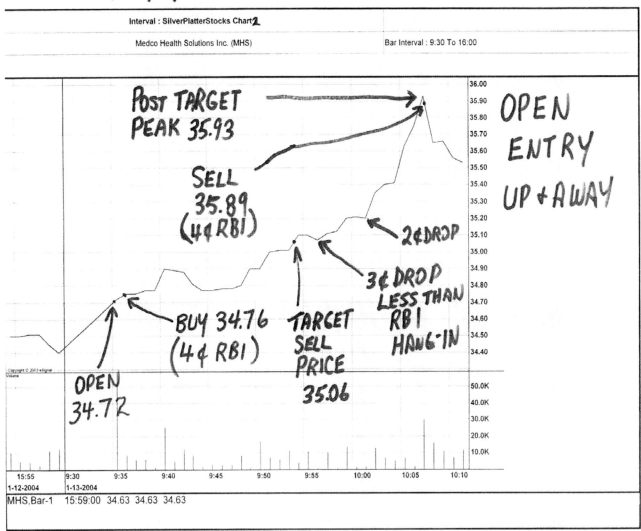

Interval : SilverPlatterStocks Chart 2

Medco Health Solutions Inc. (MHS) | Bar Interval : 9:30 To 16:00

POST TARGET PEAK 35.93

OPEN ENTRY UP & AWAY

SELL 35.89 (4¢ RBI)

2¢ DROP

3¢ DROP LESS THAN RBI HANG-IN

BUY 34.76 (4¢ RBI)

TARGET SELL PRICE 35.06

OPEN 34.72

MHS, Bar-1   15:59:00 34.63 34.63 34.63

ENTRY TIME CATEGORY: Open Entry

RBI: 4 cents

CHART PATTERN: Up & Away

EXIT SIGNAL: Post Target Peak of 35.93 Less RBI of .04 = Sell at 35.89

VOLUME: Purchase Maximum Limit: $44,994

SilverPlatter Stock Selection (Sample of P-Bounce Chart Pattern)	
Tuesday February 24 2004	
Stock Symbol:	**OPWV**
Stock Rating:	**81.9**
Previous Day Closing Price:	**14.25**
RBI:	**0.06**
V-RBI:	**0.07**
Type the Maximum $ Amount You Want to Invest:	**$10,000**
Volume Restricted Maximum $ Amount to Invest:	**$12,412**
Number of Shares You Will Buy:	**678**
'OPEN ENTRY' Price the Stock must open AT OR BELOW to qualify:	**14.43**
'BOUNCE' Price the Stock must open AT OR ABOVE to qualify:	**14.54**
Type Open Price Here (Eg 24.53) (SEE NOTE AT BOTTOM):	**14.70**
P-BOUNCE ...If Price Continues to Rise, Re-enter Each New, Higher Peak Price	
...If P-Bounce Peak Price Continues to Rise, it Can Become a Strong Parameter	
...If New, Higher Peak Price, Re-Enter Here	**14.78**
To Determine Your Bounce Bottom Point:	**14.65**
If a Bounce or P-Bounce, Type in the Actual Bounce Bottom Point:	14.25
Type in Your Buy Price Here (Eg 25.67):	14.31
If This Stock is a Play, Target Sell Price (If Blank, Type Bounce Bottom Above):	**14.43**
.....And to Determine Your Stop-Loss Price:	**14.17**
Type in Your Sell Price Here (Eg 26.90):	14.65
.....To Determine Your Profit Percentage:	**2.38%**

IMPORTANT NOTE REGARDING OPEN PRICE:
1) Wait for the 9:30 A.M. tick. 2) Then look for change in Ask, Bid & Last Prices. 3) At the Point You Have First Bid and Ask Movement & a Reasonable Bid & Ask Spread, and Volume, Mark the Corresponding Last Price as Your Open Price. (Set the Bottom of Your Graph to Show Volume.) The Stock Has NOT Opened if: 1.) There is No Trading Volume, or 2.) There is no Movement in the Bid and Ask,

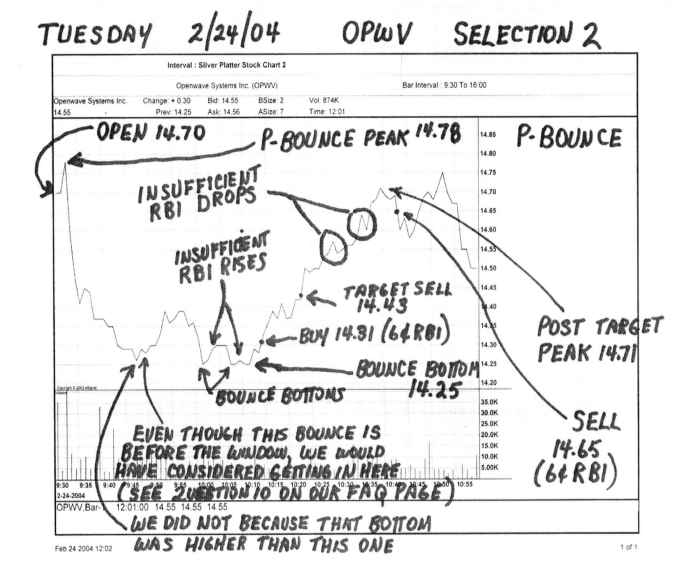

TUESDAY 2/24/04 OPWV SELECTION 2

ENTRY TIME CATEGORY: Bounce

RBI: 6 cents

CHART PATTERN: P-Bounce

EXIT SIGNAL: Post Target Peak of 14.71 Less RBI of .06 = Sell at 14.65

VOLUME: Purchase Maximum Limit: $12,412

NetPicks BreakAway or BreakDown Trading System

By Mark Soberman www.netpicks.com

This trading system is a mechanical approach to trading stocks. It works best with stocks that trade with momentum – up or down - and have some definable swings. You do not need stocks that are uptrending or downtrending steadily. Obviously in the market conditions we are seeing now, most stocks are no longer giving us those nice steady trends.

We simply want stocks that do trade with momentum in their trading swings, are volatile and trade with enough volume to enable you to get in and get out when necessary.

There are many stocks that fit that bill each and every trading day.

We'll cover how to identify the right stocks for this trading system as well as how to calculate your exact entry points and stops and even how to handle taking profits (the goal!)

The BreakAway portion of the trading system looks to buy stocks, or go "long."

The BreakDown portion of the trading system looks to short stocks.

It's advisable, if you can, to be able to trade in both directions. Obviously some traders are limited; for example, those trading with a retirement account will not be able to short. Other times certain stocks might not be available to short from your broker. However, there's always another stock and another opportunity. Clearly if you are taking trades in the direction of the broader markets, you just add on that much more opportunity for success. Trading against the market direction can work too, but it never hurts to stack the deck as much as possible in your favor.

Let's go over the trading rules and your chart set-up:

1. Use a daily chart of a stock that fits our criteria.
2. Put the Average True Range (ATR) on the chart of a 7 period and 14 period duration. This is a standard indicator that is available in virtually every stock charting package.
3. Put the stochastic (Fast) on your chart; we like to use either a 14 or 20 period. You can use the 14 if you like quicker and more frequent trade set-ups, and the 20 period if you like more confirmation and to capture potentially the more definable swings.

Here is an example of what this would look like on your workspace:

Trading Rules:

Buy/Long:

1. The Stochastic needs to read 20 or less. You are using a daily chart so you would do this in the evening after the market closes. If the stock you are trading has a stochastic of 20 or less, then you have the potential for a buy set-up.
2. Take the greater of the two Average True Range figures for the current trading day. One will be slightly larger than the next.
3. Add the Average True Range number to the high of the current trading day. This becomes your buy stop price for the next trading day.
4. Your protective stop will be a break below the set-up bar. You might want to adjust that if it's near a whole number or one of the 0.25, 0.50, 0.75 levels and put it just below.
5. Your profit target can be set several ways. You can look to take gains at a multiple of the Average True Range such as 1.0x, 1.50x, 2.0x. Or, you can look at your risk and multiply that by 1.5x to make sure you are looking to gain more than you are risking. You can raise your trade to break-even when it's gone to 1.0x, for example. In addition, should a trade set up in the opposite direction, you would exit there.

Let's look at an example from this stock: Sierra Wireless (SWIR):

On May 10, 2004, the closing high was 22.39. You take 22.39 + 2.67 (the larger of the 2 ATR readings) = 25.06 becomes your buy stop. That buy stop remains valid until filled. You can adjust it the next trading day(s) if the next trading day(s) end up calculating to a lower buy stop price, then lower your set-up. If the next day(s) doesn't give you a lower entry price, then stay with the current set-up until filled.

This trade actually did fill on May 11, as the high was 25.24, so the buy stop at 25.06 became active. The low on May 10 was 21.16 so we would have placed our stop just below the round $21 level.

At this point, you know you are risking about $4 on the trade. We want to make sure we are at least targeting an amount equal, and preferably greater, than the risk. If you took 2x the ATR of 2.67 you'd get: 2.67 x 2 = $5.34 or if you took 1.5x the risk you'd get: 4.16 x 1.50 = 6.24.

This would put our target range in between $30.40 - $31.48.

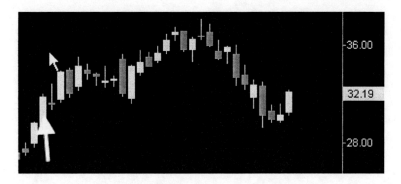

On June 8th, the stock traded through the $31 level and even higher for profits. We would have suggested reducing your risk along the way using any method you prefer; at a minimum, when the stock had gone the amount we were risking, you should have been break-even or better at that point.

You could even trail this stock until it gave a confirmed entry in the other direction (a short) and reversed the long or exited the long at that point.

Let's look at this same stock for an example of a shorting opportunity that came after the completion of this successful long.

Sell/Short:

1. The Stochastic needs to read 80 or greater. You are using a daily chart so you would do this in the evening after the market closes. If the stock you are trading has a stochastic of 80 or greater, then you have the potential for a buy set-up.
2. Take the greater of the two Average True Range figures for the current trading day. One will be slightly larger than the next.
3. Subtract the Average True Range number from the low of the current trading day. This becomes your sell short stop price for the next trading day.
4. Your protective stop will be a break above the set-up bar. You might want to adjust that if it's near a whole number or one of the 0.25, 0.50, 0.75 levels and put it just above.
5. Your profit target can be set several ways. You can look to take gains at a multiple of the Average True Range such as 1.0x, 1.50x, 2.0x. Or you can look at your risk and multiply that by 1.5x to make sure you are looking to gain more than you are risking. You can raise your trade to break-even when it's gone to 1.0x, for example. In addition, should a trade set up in the opposite direction, you would exit there.

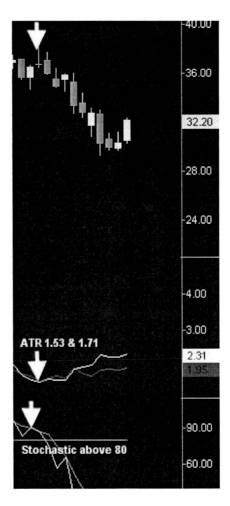

In this example of the same stock on July 6th, 2004, the set-up was there. The Stochastic was above 80, we took the low of the trading day at 36.50 – 1.71 (larger of the 2 ATRs) = 34.79 for a short. This ended up filling on July 9.

At that point we had our protective stop in above the high of the set-up day on July 6 which was 38.14, so we would put it above the xx.25 level or let's say 38.28. That means we had a risk of 38.28 – 34.79 = 3.49. We want our target to be at least that level. If we took 2x the ATR we'd get: 2 x 1.71 = 3.42 so about in line. If we take 1.5x the risk we'd have 3.49 x 1.50 = 5.24. That gives us a range of 3.42 – 5.24 for a potential target zone, which equates to: $31.37 - $29.55.

On these two days, July 14 and 15, we traded into our profit target range of 29.55 – 31.37 – actually going below that.

This stock gave us over 30% of profits with just two trades taken over a two-month timeframe.

You had a mechanical trade set-up – you knew exactly where to enter and where to exit, then you had several options on taking profits or trailing your gains.

Different traders have different styles. Some of you like to take quicker profits and exit. Others will like to take a partial profit and try to trail the balance for the bigger moves. In this case, that long from 25.06 would not have exited/reversed until the short set-up at 34.79 – that alone is a nearly 39% trading move.

NetPicks offers several trading services that incorporate this strategy and then several additional advanced features. We'll make the trade selections for you, give you the exact entry points and protective stops, and tell you where to take your profits and when to reverse.

If you are a day trader, we have a service that does the same for those who want to get in and out of the trade the same day.

For the swing traders our SwingTrader will work the same way but you will trade for several days to several weeks with active, momentum-based stocks.

All the work and research is done for you.

You can get a free two-week trial here:

http://www.netpicks.com/orderentry.html

For those of you who want to profit with the e-mini futures, we offer an e-mini day trading service that trades the S&P, Nasdaq, Dow and Russell e-minis along with the QQQ, TBonds and Eurex indexes. This is ideal for the active day trader looking to trade these markets. You can get a free trial here:

http://www.netpicks.com/dtorderentry.html

And for those of you who are trading the Forex markets, we have a new Forex trading service. We trade the EURUSD, USDCHF, GBPUSD, USDJPY, EURJPY and even the EuroFX futures contract. This service is 100% mechanical and you can take a free trial here:

http://netpicks.com/forex/fxorderentry.html

Fibonacci Trading Strategy for the Wave59 Software

(The Wave59 software is available on the Money Making Day Trading CD)

If you have studied the FibonacciSecrets™ course (www.fibonaccisecrets.com) , or are a student of Fibonacci, then you have already realized the power of using Fibonacci techniques to trade stocks and futures. Now you're ready to get started using these techniques in real time.

This manual will show you in step-by-step detail how to implement this system in the **Wave59** trading platform, as well as demonstrate a few variations using some of the unique tools found in this software package.

Wave59 is a unique trading platform. It contains many powerful trading tools not available elsewhere. These tools were once known to only a handful of floor traders and CTAs, and the algorithms behind these techniques remain a closely guarded secret to this day. Combining the analytical power behind Wave59 with the accuracy of Fibonacci will give you a distinct edge in your market operations which will allow you to trade with confidence and success.

As you've already been through the FibonacciSecrets™ manual, there's no more reason to convince you of the merits of this approach to trade selection, so let's get started!

Setting up Your Chart

The first thing that we need to do to get started using this program is to set up our chart properly. This is done easily, by clicking *File – New – Chart* . The following setup screen will appear:

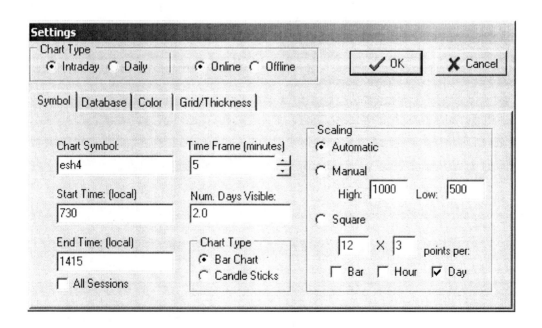

To setup your chart, simply enter the symbol to plot in "Chart Symbol" and select your time frame. In this case, I've chosen the March 2004 E-mini futures contract plotted using 5 minute bars. For daily charts, simply select "Daily" at the top. Finally, choose a scaling of "Automatic". We won't need to worry about any of the other scaling options when using this system.

Once that's done, click *OK* and you'll get a chart. Easy!

Applying our Fibonacci Ratios

The next, and most important, step is to start applying Fibonacci ratios to our chart. To do this, go *Drawing – Insert – Retracement Levels*. Your cursor will change to a small cross. Now click on the high and low of the swing you wish to calculate your retracement levels off of.

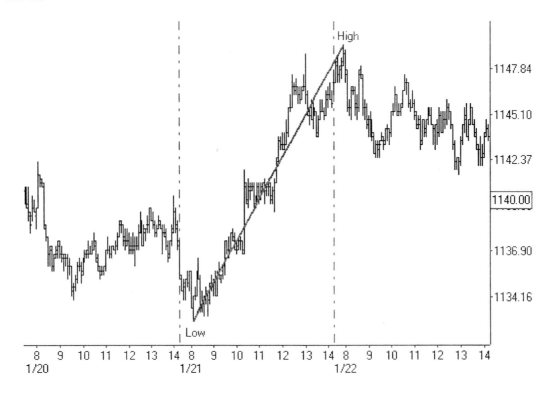

I've marked one swing on the chart above. To apply the retracement tool to the swing, simply click once on the low, then click once on the high.

You'll get the format box next:

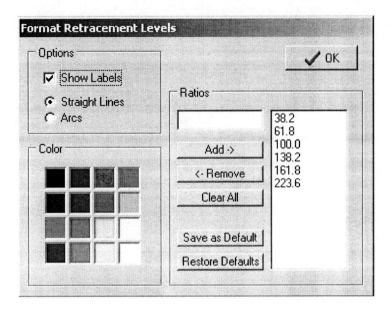

All the Fibonacci Levels we will use are shown in this box at the right. One of the benefits of using Wave59 is that you have the option of using any number of levels you wish. So if you find a particular ratio that is not working very well on your favorite market, simply delete it! You may also add custom levels that are not part of the original Fibonacci series. These ratios are all percentages, so 61.8 in the list actually means 61.8%.

Once we're happy with our selections, click *OK* and let's see the levels on our chart:

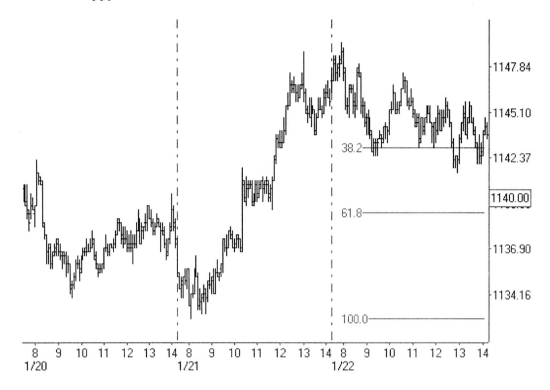

And there are the levels! Notice how the market bottomed out at the 38.2% level after the big rally. Would our system have gotten us in at this retracement level? Let's check out Stochastics and see what it said there. Click *Technical – Stochastics(Slow) – OK*. Accept the default parameters when prompted.

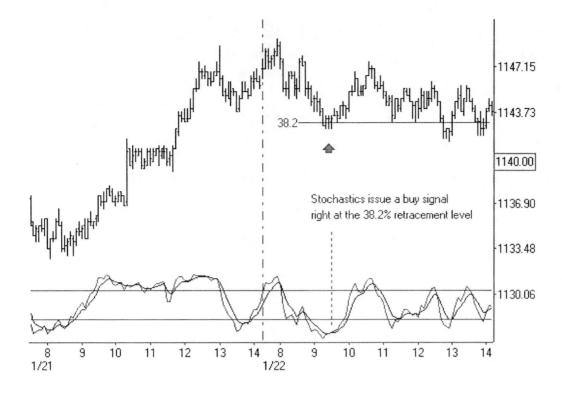

The Stochastics indicator is shown at the bottom of the chart. Note that it issued a buy signal right as the market declined into our retracement level. That caused a 5 point bounce in the market.

All the other indicators mentioned in the Fibonacci Secrets™ manual can be applied to your chart in the same way. Simply go to the "Technical" menu at the top, select the indicator you wish to add, and click *OK*.

Deleting an indicator is just as easy as adding one. You can do this by *clicking Format – Indicators*, to get the following screen:

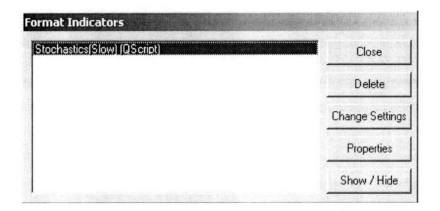

Select the indicator you wish to delete, then click "Delete". Once you click "Close", it will be removed from the chart. Note that you may also use this form to change parameter settings. So if you decide that you want your Stochastics to have a period of 5 bars instead of 14, simply come here, click "Change Settings", and you'll be on your way!

Adding a New Twist

You now know the basics on how to apply the method using this software. Now it's time to take a look at what Wave59 brings to the table in terms of it's own unique indicators. If you've looked through what's available in the Technical menu, you'll see that there are quite a few different tools available to you in this program. Some of them are very well suited to our trading method.

One such tool is the Exhaustion Bars™. To apply this indicator to your charts, go *Technical – Exhaustion Bars 1*:

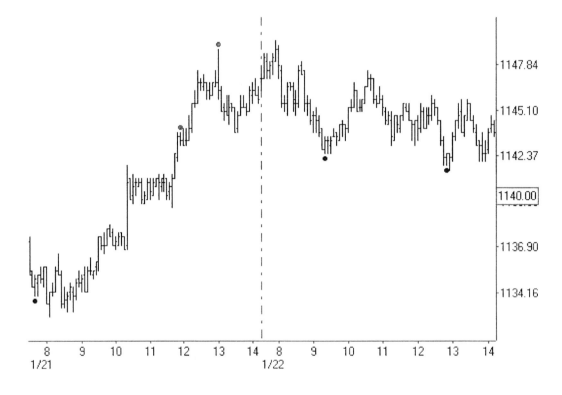

The Exhaustion Bars are the red and blue dots shown on the chart above. A red dot is a sell signal and a blue dot is a buy signal. What we want to look for is a situation where the market has moved to one of our Fibonacci retracement levels and an Exhaustion Bar signal appears. This technique is demonstrated below:

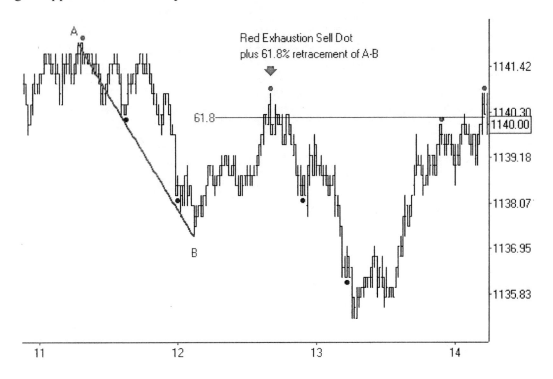

After a decline shown on the chart by the red swing A-B, the market has rallied to the 61.8% level. It hits this level, then a red Exhaustion Bar dot is triggered. This is our signal to look for a short trade. Note that we totally ignore Exhaustion Bars unless they occur right at our predefined levels.

Here's another example on a daily chart of MSFT:

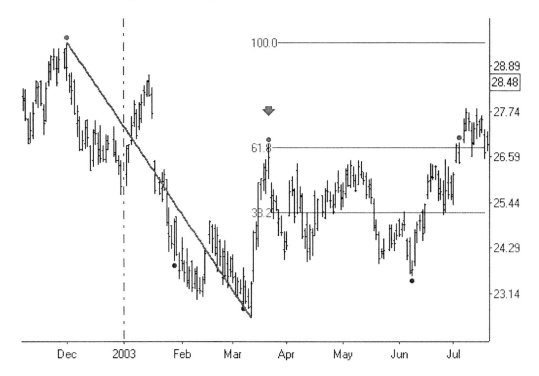

It is the exact same setup as the previous example. We have a sharp decline, then rally into our 61.8% retracement level. The Exhaustion Bar is what seals the deal.

If you look ahead into June, on this same chart, you'll find another signal:

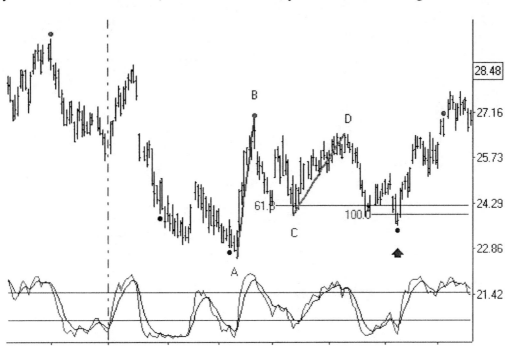

Turn your attention to the blue arrow on the chart. This is where we had our Exhaustion Bar signal. This happens as we bottom out on a cluster of ratios. One ratio (61.8%) is calculated from swing A-B and is shown in red. The other ratio is calculated from swing C-D (100%) and is shown from swing C-D. 100% is not a pure Fibonacci number, but is important in many market retracements. It is especially valid when combined with another level such as in this example. Additionally, Stochastics are giving us a buy signal here as well.

All these things happening at the same time means that this is an even more powerful signal. The market responded, and rallied 4 points in just over a month.

Shifting into High Gear (Day traders only)

Another unique tool to Wave59 is the forecaster. This is a unique approach to market timing based on cycles. The idea is that once you know what cycles the market is running on, you can run these cycles out into the future to obtain a forecast for what will happen.

Here's an example of what this looks like:

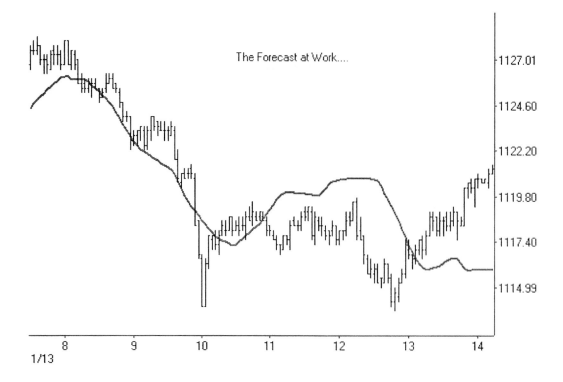

The chart above is a 5 minute bar chart of a single day in the life of the mini S&P. The red line on this chart represents our forecast of what was due to happen.

The forecast called for a decline into 10, a rally until shortly after 12, and then another decline. While not perfect, this forecast undoubtedly caught some important turns. Note that this forecast was known BEFORE the market ever even opened!

Since the forecast is just a projection of what is to happen, we still need a good entry and exit technique to be able to trade it. The strategy to use with this tool is to look ahead and spot when the major turns are in the forecast. Then use our Fibonacci tools to trade at these times of day. Let's go over an example:

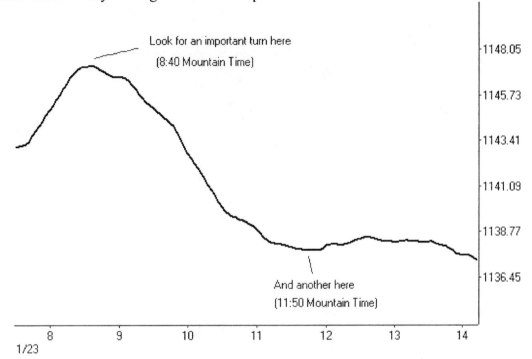

Here is what our forecast looked like before the market opened on January 23. Our forecast says there should be two major turning points this day. The most obvious one is the one at 8:40 which should lead to a large drop. The next one is at 11:50, which is not quite as good, but should also be watched. Our strategy is to wait until we are close to these times, then use our timing tools to look for a trade.

One important thing to note is that sometimes these forecasts can flip upside-down. So instead of the market making a top and declining at 8:40, we might make a bottom and then rally. The time of the turn will be the same, but we really won't know which way to go until we actually get there. If the market is falling into this time, we'll look to buy a bottom. If the market is rising into it, then we'll look to sell a top. Either way, we won't do anything unless our timing tools give us a safe setup.

Here's how this day unfolded:

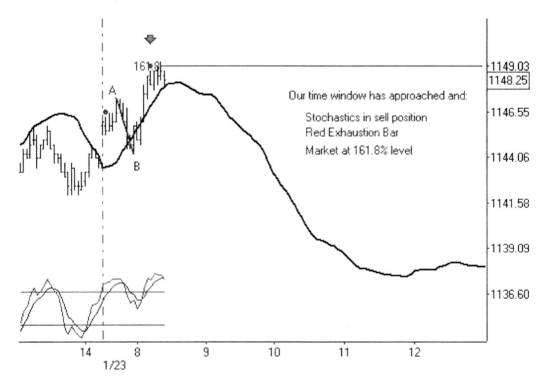

So, we've patiently waited until the market got close to our projected turning point. It's been moving up, so we are expecting a top here based on our forecast. We've just hit a 161.8% retracement from swing A-B and the market is starting to fall off. A red Exhaustion Bar dot and bearish Stochastics both support our forecast.

Let's fast forward and see what happened…

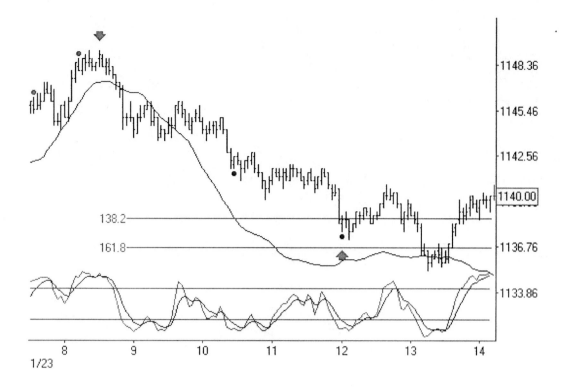

After hitting our 161.8% level, the market dropped considerably into our next forecasted turning point, shown by the second red arrow on the chart. A 10 point drop in the mini S&P is worth $500 per contract, so the tools really paid for themselves on this trade.

Our second forecasted point occurred right at a 161.8% retracement level, along with a blue Exhaustion Bar dot and bullish Stochastic reading. While not a home run trade like our first one of the day (remember our forecast didn't say this would be as good), it did go in our favor enough to make a little or at least move our stops to break-even. In all, a very successful day combining these tools!

Conclusion

This is by no means a comprehensive manual on Wave59, but it should definitely give you an idea on how you can use this software to compliment the basic FibonacciSecrets™ methods.

As an Amazing Trading Plans client, you have access to this software FREE for 30 days along with FREE intraday data from eSignal if you would like to try Wave59 in real time trading of stocks, futures and forex.

The Wave59 software along with 9 different tutorial videos is available on the CD called "Money Making Day Trading" which you should have with your Amazing Trading Plans course.

We give you plenty of time, tools and tutorials so you can learn how to potentially maximize your trading profits.

Remember to always use the basic approach that you've been taught in the FibonacciSecrets™ manual as your entry method.

Use other tools such as Exhaustion Bars, the Forecast, and Stochastics as the confirming indicators to the Fibonacci ratios. If you keep track of the direction of the main trend, and are careful to manage your trade with protective stops, then there's nothing stopping you from being successful trading with this approach.

CONCLUSION

By Stephen Pierce

The trading methods which have just been described to you here may seem either basic or advanced, depending on your level of trading experience.

Whatever your perception is of these amazing trading plans, the one thing we want you to know is …THEY WORK!

We suggest that you try them all on paper, starting first with the plan that has the greatest appeal to you. See for yourself how effective these strategies are in stocks, futures and forex.

Don't just take our word for it or the word of the contributors to this body of work. Put these trading plans to the test and see what difference it can make in your trading.

Once you start trading it on paper successfully, then you can start using these amazing trading plans in your real money account… and when the profits start rolling in, be sure to write us and share your success story with us and what plan you are using.

We feel certain that this collection of trading strategies can be more than informative and be truly impactful and transformational. So we look forward to hearing about how much you love these amazing trading plans and the positive impact they have had on your life.

God Bless YOU and YOURS,

Stephen Pierce

NOTES:

NOTES:

NOTES:

NOTES:

NOTES:

NOTES:

NOTES:

NOTES:

NOTES:

_____

_____

_____

_____

_____

_____

_____

_____

_____

_____

_____

_____

_____

_____

_____

_____

_____

_____

_____

_____

_____

NOTES:

NOTES:

_____

_____

_____

_____

_____

_____

_____

_____

_____

_____

_____

_____

_____

_____

_____

_____

_____

_____

_____

_____

NOTES:

NOTES:

_____

_____

_____

_____

_____

_____

_____

_____

_____

_____

_____

_____

_____

_____

_____

_____

_____

_____

_____

NOTES:

NOTES:

_____

_____

_____

_____

_____

_____

_____

_____

_____

_____

_____

_____

_____

_____

_____

_____

_____

_____

_____

_____

_____

_____

NOTES:

NOTES:

_____

_____

_____

_____

_____

_____

_____

_____

_____

_____

_____

_____

_____

_____

_____

_____

_____

_____

_____

NOTES:

NOTES:

NOTES: